CRITICISM
SPECULATIVE AND ANALYTICAL ESSAYS

THE UNIVERSITY OF WISCONSIN PRESS
MADISON, MILWAUKEE, AND LONDON 1968

SPECULATIVE
AND
ANALYTICAL
ESSAYS

CRITICISM

EDITED BY
L. S. DEMBO

Published by
The University of Wisconsin Press
Box 1379, Madison, Wisconsin 53701
The University of Wisconsin Press, Ltd.
27–29 Whitfield Street, London, W.1
Copyright © 1968 by the
Regents of the University of Wisconsin
All rights reserved
Printed in
the United States of America
by NAPCO, Inc.
Milwaukee, Wisconsin
Library of Congress
Catalog Card Number 68–9830

The articles
in this volume
originally appeared in *Contemporary Literature*
Summer, 1968

FOR BLAKE NEVIUS

PREFACE

When plans were initiated for the Modern Criticism number of *Contemporary Literature* (Summer, 1968), in which these studies first appeared, it was assumed that the articles would bear no particular relation to one another. By the time the issue was completed, however, a subject had emerged, and even though the contributors did not necessarily engage in a full debate, they at least dealt in their own ways with common problems. Murray Krieger and Northrop Frye presented papers on interpretation and evaluation at the Modern Language Association meeting in December 1967. E. D. Hirsch, Jr., was present and accepted an invitation to continue the discussion in print. Wayne Shumaker had already submitted an essay that treated one aspect of literary interpretation. All but one of the remaining articles dealt with European speculative critics for whom interpretation and evaluation took place on a level that often far transcended the limits of the work itself. Finally, Richard Foster took a dissenting position to the classroom study of methodology and theories, *per se.* Hence the issue virtually became a book.

I am most indebted in this enterprise to George Stavros, for his services as Managing Editor of *Contemporary Literature*, and to Mrs. Cyrena Pondrom, of the Comparative Literature Department of the University of Wisconsin, for her many invaluable suggestions.

L. S. D.

Madison
Spring, 1968

CONTENTS

CRITICISM
SPECULATIVE AND ANALYTICAL ESSAYS

INTRODUCTION AND PERSPECTIVE

I

When R. S. Crane proposed the idea of a critique of criticism based on the careful examination of "conceptual schemes" and "methodologies," he was perhaps, like Kant, seeking a Copernican revolution. Or again, instead of merely looking at the stars, he wished to investigate the telescope. Like Analytical Philosophy, critical pluralism seeks to define, though in logical if not epistemological terms, the means of perception and conception, which it takes to be prior to all other inquiries into statements about objective reality. Crane's approach is in a sense a formalization and a version of modern critics' general concern with self-awareness, of the need for scrutinizing one's presuppositions, attitudes, and responses—the "categories" of one's own mind and of others—in order to arrive at an understanding of the true state of things. The current interest in literary criticism as a legitimate and rewarding subject in itself is perhaps a part of the Kantian legacy. There is, of course, a difference between "Kantian" method and the philosophy of Kant, and in pursuing the former one comes to realize that differences in philosophic presuppositions are frequently the crucial ones in critical argument, when critics are speaking on different levels or at cross-purposes, as well as when they are engaged in authentic debate.

The position papers on literary evaluation and interpretation delivered by Murray Krieger and Northrop Frye at the Modern Language Association meeting in December 1967, and published here, along with original contributions by E. D. Hirsch, Jr., and Wayne Shumaker, point up the fact that brilliance need not end in persuasion. The problem of evaluation, seemingly capable only of logical and

3

not substantive solution, is a catalytic one, for, in a sense, its discussion requires that the critic formulate and express a range of fundamental beliefs.

Murray Krieger, for example, presents an argument that is largely Kantian in substance if not method. In asserting the inseparability of interpretation and value judgment, he agrees with E. D. Hirsch, Jr., that "the perspective that determines what we would have the work become in order to make sense of its parts is in turn determined by our prior notion, implicit or explicit, of what we will value in poetry—or value as poetry." The argument here is for the essential apriority of both interpretation and value judgment itself. The critic sees only what his "categories of vision" permit him to see, and the result is that "as critics we are dealing no longer with the work itself, intrinsically, in its own terms, but with our conceptual terms to which a partial and distorted abstraction from the work is adapted."

Crane, Krieger notes, was also concerned with the problem of apriority, but ended in a circular conception when he tried to formulate the principles on which an inductive criticism could be based. Krieger denies the validity of Hirsch's idea of "intrinsic genre" ("not quite the work itself, since the work can be translated into it, yet as genre not broad enough to include any other work") and "intentional object" (the work as "a single, determinate entity" that has grown out of "the author's intended or willed meaning"). He asks whether these are not merely verbal entities designed to give interpretation a privileged status. This does not mean, however, that Krieger abandons the possibility of objective correspondences among critical views of a work. He insists, paradoxically, that "the critic . . . must still manage to 'anchor' the axiological to the observable features" of the literary object. On the one hand, in his attempt to characterize the work, the critic cannot really escape what Hirsch called the "hermeneutic circle"; he can do little more than "bend" his "languauge and methods to grope after" the work or "throw his own self-enclosed circle against all comers in hopes of seeming more adequate to his data. On some rare occasions he may even change someone's mind or be persuaded to change his own."

On the other hand, the work of art is not precisely a *ding-an-sich* but a force that breaks in upon one's subjective categories, "through the self-sufficient insulation of our visionary circles," and imposes objective control upon the reader:

Though the work seems to exist for us only as our categories permit it to be defined, only as our commonplace, generic symbols reduce and distort its unique symbolic structure—still there must be something in the work as it must exist (or subsist?), on its own, outside our categorical structures and symbols. This something can force our structures and symbols to work radical transformations upon themselves, in response to their own commands, as it were, though prompted from beyond their autonomous realm.

The problem seems to be, however, that the combination of subjective and objective elements yields a different conception of the whole work to different readers. Therefore complete agreement among critics about the essence of the work remains—and must always remain—beyond reach. This is not to say that one should not attempt to be precise in comparing his vision with those of others; indeed his own view will probably be modified in the process. Still, one's experience with the work, and one's description of it, are necessarily partial. "There is no way of getting at the force" which is the work of art, writes Krieger, "—despite radical disagreements about its nature —except through our radically diverse, autonomous experiences of it, even as our judgments of these experiences must be modified through dialogue." He concludes by saying,

Those of us whose impatience leads them to introduce systematically controlled, firmly generic criteria from the outside in order to eliminate the subjective angle of vision are deceiving themselves about the positive nature of the results they look for. The force which is the work itself lives only in those singular visions and in their mutual modifications by men honestly trying to look, and to move, beyond their own limitations. . . .

Because Krieger emphasizes the "autonomous" quality of each man's experience of literature, his view leads essentially to an epistemological scepticism, whatever the qualifications he tries to give it. Are rational discourse, objectivity, conceptualization, and the knowledge they provide any more futile in the apprehension of literature than of nature itself? Northrop Frye begins his essay by arguing that he cannot discuss the problem on Krieger's level and, by implication, that he is unconcerned with epistemology. The truth is, however, that he has taken epistemology for granted—that for him there is no question that valid knowledge of literature is as possible as valid knowledge of nature. Indeed, those familiar with the *Anatomy of Criticism* can appreciate that Frye is, loosely speaking, as much a

Realist as Krieger is an Idealist; the central premise of the *Anatomy* is that the order of nature, discoverable by the scientist, is recapitulated in the order of literature (taken as a whole), discoverable by the critic through inductive reasoning and observation.

For Frye, then, it is evaluation alone that is subjective, although one's sense of value is refined in direct proportion to the extent of one's knowledge. Actually even here Frye refuses to see judgment as being simply subjective, and he presents a view of "taste" as a social-historical, as much as a psychological, phenomenon:

Today we still have, despite the linguists, distinctions between standard and substandard speech, and a corresponding distinction, though one quite different in its application, between standard and substandard writing. The critic who fights his way through to some kind of intuitive feeling for what literary conventions are accepted in his society becomes a representative of the good taste of his age.

But the crux of Frye's argument is the distinction between the tasks of the evaluating critics, who "review contemporary books and plays," and the literary scholars, who are "trying to organize our knowledge of our past culture." "The fundamental critical act," he writes, "is the act of recognition, seeing what is there. . . ." Thus while he concedes that there may be some merit in Krieger's view that one can not really distinguish between interpretation and evaluation, at least in the case of the individual critic, he maintains that in the long run the separation is inexorable: "When a critic interprets, he is talking about his poet; when he evaluates, he is talking about himself, or, at most, about himself as a representative of his age."

Both Krieger and Frye are provocative if not definitive in their arguments. One senses that "interpretation" does not mean quite the same thing for one as it does for the other. Frye's term *knowledge* does not distinguish, for example, between the kinds of results possible to literary inquiry. Perhaps apropos here is Crane's attempt in an early essay (later repudiated) to point out the difference between historical and critical interpretation:

whereas . . . the critic . . . can center his attention solely, if he wishes, on particular masterpieces considered as organic wholes and utilize all the resources of esthetic analysis in an attempt to seize as much as possible of their distinguishing structures and styles, the historian . . . must restrict his characterizations of individual literary works to the traits . . . which serve to link these works to another in the particular causal sequence he is trying to exhibit.[1]

When Frye speaks of knowledge, he clearly has "historical" interpretation in mind, whereas Krieger has "critical." If Frye does not really answer Krieger's point that critical interpretation is subjective, Krieger does not, I feel, really discredit Frye's pragmatic faith that historical knowledge, whether of nature or literature, can be true and necessary. To Krieger's question, "Who indeed can look on beauty bare?," Frye might well have answered, "Why, Euclid alone."

E. D. Hirsch, Jr., sets out to resolve what he takes to be the fundamental disagreement between Krieger and Frye—that between the "separatist," who insists upon the distinction between "the serious study of literature" and "mere ideology or taste," and the "anti-separatist," who finds the distinction "undesirable or philosophically naive." The very title of his essay, "Literary Evaluation as Knowledge," indicates that he disagrees both with Frye's point that evaluation is not the proper function of the critic and with Krieger's implication that, finally, no "knowledge" about art is authentic. It is not surprising, then, that while he should accept Krieger's relegation of him to Frye's camp, Hirsch should spend the bulk of his essay arguing for what he finds valid in Krieger's anti-separatist position.

For Hirsch the inseparability of description and judgment is an epistemological fact demonstrated by Kant in his aesthetic theories. Kant conceived of value as "belonging to the very essence of a work of art. . . . The aesthetic value of anything cannot be dissociated from the thing itself as an object of aesthetic contemplation." Hirsch's point is that "no description of literature can properly escape judgments of value, since Kant's argument about beauty would apply to all the values which belong to the work as a necessary property of its being perceived." Hirsch believes that the so-called "instrumentalist" theory of value, justified by Kant, resolves the dichotomy between subjectivity and universality. Beauty or value is relational; an object "is inherently beautiful because it is or ought to be universally beautiful to mankind. For the experience of beauty is subjective; its 'objectivity' consists in the universality of the subjective experience." Hirsch, then, breaks with Krieger when he goes on to emphasize not the basic subjectivity of critical response, but rather the universality made possible

---

[1] "History versus Criticism," in *The Idea of the Humanities, and Other Essays Critical and Historical* (Chicago and London, 1967), II, 10.

by a "common sense" (Kant). (Actually, he finds himself closest, with reservations, to the anti-separatist position of René Wellek.)

It is precisely by the idea of a common sense that Kant explains the possibility of cognition itself and its intimate connection to value. The "objects of cultural experience, no less than those of primary sensation, are constituted by the mental organization of the perceiver"; therefore if "we are to have a shared cultural object of cognition, we must also have a 'common sense' with respect to that object." Thus "our very cognition of a shared cultural object presupposes a shared system of feelings and attitudes with respect to it."

Following Kant, Hirsch argues that "different meanings could have *existence* only through the different constitutive mental sets which sponsored both the meanings and their correspondent affects," a principle that at once points up the relation between meaning and value and emphasizes the subjective nature of both. On the other hand, the principle of "universal subjective validity" "requires that the correctness (universal shareability) of the cognition be established, not just the correlation between cognition and value." Hirsch finds Kant's answer to what constitutes "correctness" inadequate and he tries to clarify the issue by distinguishing between necessary and unnecessary value judgments, the former being a part of one's cognition of the work. Although it is true that in fact the "only universally valid cognition of a work of art is that which is constituted by the kind of subjective stance adopted in its creation," "other attitudes toward the work are obviously possible." Hirsch attempts to demonstrate that the application of an "alien subjective stance"—that is, one different from the author's at the time of creation—"does not necessarily destroy or distort the subjective stance which constitutes the meaning of a work. The integrity of the work with its attendant values can be preserved while judgment is passed upon it."

This belief, of course, seems to be in direct opposition to Krieger's scepticism; consistently enough, Hirsch concludes by asserting that there is no reason for making art the object of a mystique and that it is in the best interests of humanistic studies to view the values of literature as being "continuous with all other shared values of human culture."

As a disquisition in aesthetics, Hirsch's article attempts a resolution of the problems of interpretation and value judgment on essentially philosophic grounds. It counters Krieger's point that critical interpretation is "singular vision" (something Frye did not really set out to do), but it does not try to invalidate Frye's practical distinction between interpretation and evaluation. In his overall view Hirsch is not an absolute anti-separatist and his argument is actually but an attempt to concede what can be conceded to the anti-separatist position. His final belief is that while cognition includes certain kinds of value judgments, it does not include all of them, and that external judgment—separate from interpretation—is both possible and justifiable.

Wayne Shumaker not only shares Frye's belief in the validity of the empirical study of literature, but he is sufficiently optimistic about the present state of critical knowledge to make certain "modest proposals" he believes are necessary to check the critic's pride. An account of the criteria for relevant evidence, his discussion attempts, among other things, to clarify the problem of meaning, particularly in regard to the author's intention:

When a writer is fully caught up in his work, he senses fitnesses for which, unless his mind is exceptionally analytic, he feels it unnecessary to construct elaborate justifications. . . . The critic, whose specialty I think should be understanding and explaining, can sometimes perceive the necessity and in the course of doing so discover a valid but unintended meaning. Although at times his subject may be precisely the author's conscious purposes, it need not always be that. . . .

Shumaker is especially disturbed by what he feels are excessive investigations of historical backgrounds in which the author is assumed to be conversant with all the erudition of his age. In short, historical information is not always relevant to critical interpretation. Despite this distinction between learning and perception, Shumaker, like Frye, is unconcerned with the problem of *apriority* in criticism. Or better, since he believes the ideal reader should, on his initial contact with the work, present "a *tabula rasa* upon which it may impress its meanings and patterns," *a priori* for him is associated only with irrelevant knowledge and may be transcended.

II

The criticism of Georg Lukács, Roland Barthes, Menno Ter Braak, and Friedrich Gundolf elevates the problem of interpretation and evaluation to a new dimension. Each of the European writers, as will be seen in essays by Stephen G. Nichols, Jr., Hugh M. Davidson, E. M. Beekman, and René Wellek, possesses what amounts to a metaphysical vision of the critical act. It is true that Frye, in the *Anatomy*, views literature in terms of a structure that is, finally, metaphysical, but it does not issue from any particular ideology, nor does it endow the ideal critic with any qualities but those of "objectivity" and analytical rigor.

In his discussion of Lukács, Nichols finds in Marxism the critic's philosophic basis for transforming literary works into historical objects, a part of the dialectics of history. Irrelevant to this approach are the intentions of the author and the experiences of the reader; what is important is the *Weltanschauung* determined by the astute Marxist critic. "Since literature bears witness to the totality of society and its patterns of development," writes Nichols, interpreting Lukács' reasoning, "criticism can do no less than to reveal the full perspective, the potentiality of the literary object it studies." In short, "the perspective created by the description" is more important than "the independent experience of the work." The difficulty, Nichols argues, is that the so-called objective elements to be singled out by the observant critic "do not come naturally from consideration of the text itself, but are value judgments whose truth derives from their dialectical presentation by the critic," and it is the critic alone who is responsible for defining the historical context or what constitutes objective criteria. What seemingly begins in a broad objectivity actually ends in a kind of solipsism. Lukács "assumes the self-evidence of history as *perceived by* Hegel, Marx, Engels, and Lenin," but the fact that he "does not stand by himself in the middle of his interpretive circle does not alter the essentially solipsistic nature of his relationship to the work."

It is clear from Nichols' analysis that Lukács bears a relation to the study of literature similar to that of a Hegel or a Spengler to the study of history. The critic seeks to provide a "reality," in terms of an *a priori* vision that far transcends the limited interpretations of the authentic empiricist. It is one thing to assert, as does Shumaker, that meaning is not always limited to the author's intention; quite another to reestablish meaning on a level that makes all intention but the critic's irrelevant.

We are faced with a similar "expansion of focus," to use Nichols' expression, in the criticism of Roland Barthes, a chief figure in the recent French *Nouvelle Critique*. In his famous controversy with the scholar Raymond Picard, as Davidson tells us, Barthes attempted to justify his own symbolic approach against charges of subjectivity, obsession with sexuality, and ideological impressionism, among others, by defining a *critique idéologique* to be set in opposition to the *critique universitaire*. Ideological criticism, that in which the critic uses "one of the principal intellectual languages now being spoken" (Marxism, psychoanalysis, existentialism, etc.), encompasses two differing methodologies: referral of the work to an external system of ideas and concentration upon the work itself. Barthes claims this latter method, called the *critique d'interprétation*, for himself and other critics such as Poulet and Richard. Like the American New Critics, Barthes believes that literature is a special kind of language, essentially symbolic but multiple in its significance. Still arguing against the academic criticism of Picard, in which a work is fixed in its historical and literal contexts, Barthes sees literature as being open to perpetual interpretation and asserts that the aim of the critic is (in the words of Davidson) to express the "sense that modern man can give to the works of the past."

The very definition of the work changes [writes Barthes]: it is no longer an historical fact; it becomes an anthropological fact, since no history exhausts it. The variety of senses does not depend on a relativistic view of human customs; it designates, not an inclination of society to error, but a disposition of the work to the openness; the work possesses at one and the same time several senses for reasons of structure, not because of weakness on the part of those who read it.

For Barthes, the function of the critic, then, is actually to make a "second writing with the first writing of the work," explains Davidson. What is crucial is that the critic "must respect the symbolic character of the literary language"—that is, write in a language that is harmonious with that of the work. Poetical and critical styles coalesce; "the reflexive meta-language of criticism accompanies and extends creative activity, so that now there is only one kind of writing."

Barthes, like Lukács, is indeed an "ideological critic" if, by that expression, we mean one who moves beyond interpretation to re-creation, whether in terms of an external system or a structure based on one's personal insight. It is not surprising that both these writers, who would turn criticism into a science of interpretation, are ultimately open to charges of subjectivism. A frankly subjectivistic critic, challenging, like Barthes, the academic or traditional establishment, is Menno Ter Braak, a Dutch figure whose life and work are here described by E. M. Beekman. "Championing the poet against the plurality of the burghers . . . the iconoclastic writer against the aesthetes and the formalist critics . . . and the lone *honnête homme* against the profusion of political ideologists, Ter Braak adhered consistently throughout his life to the doctrine of individuality." Beekman goes on to cite Kierkegaard's definition of the ideal subjective thinker—relevant to Ter Braak's own viewpoint as well as to Ter Braak himself:

> Every human being must be assumed in essential possession of what essentially belongs to being a man. The task of the subjective thinker is to transform himself into an instrument that clearly and definitely expresses in existence whatever is essentially human.

It is Beekman's point that Ter Braak was always the spokesman for "existence," concrete reality, and process against abstractionism, convention, and fixity. Just as for Barthes a literary work was never complete, but capable of endless interpretation, so Ter Braak saw his own work as part of a process:

> One must not be able to finish since it sobers a book—that formal and dignified burgher—with the semblance of completion, of totality, of leaving behind, or it induces a sleep of burgher-contentment, to have completed something. This paper burgher, built from every type of word and constructed according to a certain syntax, remains invitingly behind, waiting; waiting for whom?

To be emphasized, however, is the notion that subjectivity, far from being a weakness, is a positive virtue. Thus Beekman tells us that for Ter Braak the objective critics had no relationship to art, yet claimed "to have the 'correct method' for interpretation in the hermetically closed domain of Beauty, since return to nature means for them the destruction of that domain wherein they became such excellent officials." For this kind of critic art is merely "a collection of isolated objects which are . . . judged with the presumption of infallibility"; he is, in brief, devoted to "the abstract product of art." In truth, one "must suspect hierarchies of values and autonomous principles since nothing is absolute or isolated in the fluid relativity of the process of existence." Ter Braak was openly an impressionistic critic and there is nothing unusual in his admiration for Nietzsche nor in his kinship, pointed out by Beekman, with Kierkegaard. The wonder is that he is so little known in the United States, for he is clearly a part of a major trend in contemporary thought and criticism.

German criticism, of course, is well known for its tendency to work in terms of large constructions or central theses that are chiefly speculative or derived from personal insight. Characteristic is the work of Friedrich Gundolf (1880–1931), here analyzed and evaluated by René Wellek. Originally a member of the Stefan George circle, Gundolf shared a concern for "restitution of hero-worship, a belief in the exemplary power of the great men in history." His first, and what Wellek believes is possibly his best, book of literary history, *Shakespeare und der deutsche Geist*, conceives of "the whole history of German literature from the seventeenth century to the Romantic movement . . . as a struggle to approach Shakespeare: his language, his poetry, his tragic or comic feeling, not only through translations and adaptations or critical estimates but in creative competition and in drama as well as in the lyric or the novel." According to Wellek, the book, except in tone, is in the tradition of "*Geistesgeschichte*" and relies too heavily on the "dualistic typologies of the German tradition emanating from Schiller's treatise on naive and sentimental poetry; on the contrasts between classical and romantic, Apollonian and Dionysiac art," and the like. (Interestingly enough, this is precisely the kind of a *priori* method that R. S. Crane discerned in the criticism of John Crowe Ransom, which concerned itself with the dualism of "structure" and "texture.") In *Goethe*, Wellek writes, Gundolf sought "the evocation and construction of a 'figure' (*Gestalt*) which is conceived as a union of life and work." This approach presupposes that the artist has an "inborn entelechy" and fulfills "a predetermined fate." "Goethe appears as an 'original man in a derivative world' . . . constantly struggling for an assertion of the inner sources of his being against the outer impact of civilization." Gundolf describes his character in terms of "*Urerlebnisse*" ("everything religious, titanic, and erotic") and "*Bildungserlebnisse*" ("the German past, the encounter with Shakespeare, with classical antiquity, with Italy, with the Orient and with the whole German society"). Influenced as he was by Dilthey's theory of *Erlebnis* (experience), Gundolf, in Wellek's opinion, could not escape a psychologism in which immediacy, spontaneity, and sincerity were the chief criteria of value. Wellek cites Gundolf's predilection for Bergsonian ideas and in fact we are reminded here of Ter Braak's suspicion of "hierarchies of values . . . since nothing is absolute or isolated in the fluid relativity of the process of existence." Gundolf and Ter Braak share a concept of art and life in which "becoming" is the distinguishing characteristic. As we have seen, the idea of process also enters into Barthes' thinking.

After discussing Gundolf's psychology of language and his evaluation of Kleist, Wellek concludes that while one cannot help seeing Gundolf as propagandist for George's creed of hero worship and as a participant in the "whole tradition of the irrationalistic *Lebensphilosophie*," one must admire him for his break with "the dreary positivism of the nineteenth century," for his "assertion, new in its time and place, of absolute values in poetry" (in the spiritual sense), and for his "concentration on what matters in the poets he studied." The redeeming qualities that Wellek finds in Gundolf seem to be analogous to those that Davidson found in Barthes and Beekman in Ter Braak. Each of these speculative critics challenged academic authority or more specifically pedantic historicism, and introduced a new dimension to literary study. How meaningful that dimension is depends, ultimately, on the temperamental and intellectual predisposition of the reader.

III

In establishing principles for the teaching of literary criticism, Richard Foster sets himself against the whole methodological approach. He asserts that

emphasis on methodology and relativistic objectivism, because they are opposed to sensibility and are thus the potential enemies of literature and literary experience, should be relegated to their properly dependent, ancillary, and at most corrective roles.

"Sensibility" does not mean for Foster mere impressionism. Rather he seems to be arguing against the kind of analysis that he purports was made by Aristotle: "definition, fixity, authority, drill, detail, and the mechanics of sorting and storing." He prescribes what amounts to a comparative course based on

first, the intellectual principle of continual comparison and contrast of critical statements; second, the axiological principle of testing the inherent interest and worth of those statements by the trial of literature-as-experienced; and third, the—let us say "economic"—principle that from each critic's work shall be distilled answers to the questions, What are the critic's conceptions of the nature of literature, the function of literature, and the form of the creative process?

It is essential to Foster that the course be "humanistic" rather than "scientific." In literary criticism, he concludes, "much knowledge, at least knowledge about such things as critical theories and methods, can be far more dangerous . . . than a little or none at all."

This view is, of course, not pluralistic but eclectic. As noted, methodology is the chief concern of Crane, whose whole theory presupposes the integrity of individual systems of thought. Foster's suggestions are related to the teaching of undergraduates, and one can perhaps sympathize with his desire to take an experiential approach in which critics are made to "debate" one another across the centuries, are subjected to the students' personal responses, and are given hypothetical problems outside their normal range of thought. Nonetheless, critical conceptions do emerge from certain historical and philosophic conditions and they do require historical and philosophic study if they are to be understood in the terms in which they were formulated. Accordingly, inquiry into "critical theories and methods" need be no more "anti-humanistic" than inquiry into the form of a novel or the development of a poem. In any case, I know the reader will find provocative enough the following versions of critical speculation and analysis.

L. S. Dembo

LITERARY ANALYSIS AND EVALUATION—
AND THE AMBIDEXTROUS CRITIC

Murray Krieger

1

Ever since the critical revolutions we usually trace to T. S. Eliot and
I. A. Richards, theorists and practical critics—despite their self-
conscious methodological concerns—have often confounded problems
of description and problems of prescription, problems of fact and
problems of value. On the one hand there is the "reading" of the
literary work, the analysis or interpretation of it; on the other hand
there is the judgment we make of the aesthetic worth of that which
we have laid out. But this two-handedness, with its sensible division
of labor, has often been blurred into a confusing ambidexterity. Theoretical neatness may lead to an analytic separation of function; but
the limits have—and often profitably—been overrun in practice. Perhaps only the rigorous apriorist, too dedicated to his trim lines of logical distinction that experience defies, need lament. But I must not
allow my own judgment of these theoretical issues to intrude itself
until later.

From the beginnings of that increasingly antique movement we
have been calling New Criticism, the very definition of what we call
poetry—as well as our attempt to define that single work before us—
has been tinged by value considerations. Have our critics been asking,
"What are these things one (anyone?) calls poems?" or rather have
they not really been asking, "What had these things better be before

_____

This essay is an expanded version of a paper read to the General Topics
I (Poetics and Literary Theory) Group of the Modern Language Association in
December 1967. Besides other changes and additions, Section IV has been
inserted into the version I originally presented.

we honor them with the title, 'poem'?" On single works have they been asking, like the scientist, "What is the nature of the workings of this entity before me?" or rather, like the prepossessed guardian of the heavenly empire, "What are its obligations to work in given ways for me if I am to allow it entrance?" As humanists, we should have to be pleased that such questions are not kept rigorously distinct, as we confess our inability to restrict ourselves to the first kind, the strictly descriptive.

Even someone as obsessed with the hegemony of scientism as was the early I. A. Richards could not allow his devotion to the supposed facts of neurology to overcome his greater obsession with the varying worth of poems, those supposed neutral stimuli of responses—stimuli, however, that turn out utterly value-ridden before he is done with them. We can recall his desperate attempt, in *Principles of Literary Criticism* (1925), to disdain any departure from the quantitative— his desperate attempt, that is, to reduce all poetic value to poetic response and to reduce all poetic response to response in general: to the number of neurological impulses being aroused and satisfied, or at least sustained. How fervently Richards derided the most modest qualitative suggestion; how ascetically he remained faithful to his Benthamite calculation, refusing to proceed beyond his neutral (neural) quantitative analysis. But, alas, how self-deceptively he was at each crucial point seduced into happy inconsistency by his own critical powers as sensitive reader.

So, as he argued from the number of impulses (and of opposed impulses) organized in the reader to the stimuli in the provocative object, he enabled himself to distinguish between poems organized (as he put it) by inclusion and poems organized by exclusion, finally determining that those works controlled by irony had their inclusive- ness so expanded as to become poetry "of the highest order." And, contrary to his descriptive and psychological intentions, he was led to objective discriminations among the features *in* poems, features that are irreducibly aesthetic. How short a step it is from here to making the definition of *true* poetry an honorific one, to calling the poetry of exclusion, with its service of the will and its consequent failure of imagination, a mere pseudo-poetry or rhetoric in disguise, with the valued title of poetry reserved for the inclusive work, expressive of many-sided complexities. This is just the short step, occasionally sug- gested if not taken by Richards himself, which was taken, openly and firmly, by his followers—say, William Empson, Allen Tate, Cleanth Brooks. Their critical analysis is aimed at discovering whether its object deserves to be called a poem, whether it measures up to the high standard of their normative definition, so that with them the act of evaluation automatically, perhaps unconsciously, accompanies— nay, defines and becomes identical with—the act of analysis. These critics, with Richards, inherit their blurring procedure from their master, Coleridge, much of whose work seems singularly dedicated to discovering in the literature with which he deals the presence of "imagination," the alchemical faculty (or quality) that transmutes discourse into poetry and earns it that noble denomination.

Thus one can trace in recent criticism the "Platonic" methodo- logical tradition which the late R. S. Crane and his fellow neo- Aristotelians disdainfully refer to as "critical monism," as they see it, for example, in the "irony" of Richards, the "ambiguity" of Empson, the "tension" of Tate, the "paradox" of Brooks. The neo-Aristotelians are complaining about the aprioristic establishment of a single poetic characteristic and the use of it not only to define a work as poetry but also, in the same act, automatically to judge it as a valuable example of that high literary mode. They lament the theoretical construction of the Procrustean bed, a practice from which a limited collection of most favored poems emerges, as all but those works responsive to this treatment come to be excluded from the canon of the very best or are admitted only after suffering major distortions. Nevertheless the neo- Aristotelians themselves, anxious to substitute pluralism for monism, many differentiated species for a monolithic poetry, end by falling prey to a similar confusion between the empirical and the a priori, between description and judgment. With a circularity that belies their announced inductive intention, they must end by judging the single work by its efficacy in fulfilling its final cause, the working-power of the peculiar pre-defined species which their analytic description has found it (or trimmed it, forced it) to fit.

This circularity seems universally indulged in by our analytically inclined critics, from so-called contextualists to neo-Aristotelians, whatever their other differences and their vain attempts to evade such circularity and to work toward what they would like to think of as inductive method. For the a priori categories are in control, con- stituting what they see by limiting how they see. The categories define their subject and erect value criteria for admission, so that for the work to attain the definition is for it to qualify as a valued individual in a valued class. The work comes to be discovered, defined, and val- ued as poetry only by way of a pre-existing generic characteristic which the critic began by adopting as his perspective glass to envision it.

Indeed, it should by now seem clear that these critics are doubly guilty of circularity. First, there is the evaluative circularity I have been pointing out, the judging of the work by its conformity to a generic trait or set of traits which are the very ones that have been used to define goodness in poetry, or really to define poetry or a kind of poetry as an honorific class. But, more extremely, there is circularity even in the value-free interpretation of works. Here we enter the "hermeneutic circle" which E. D. Hirsch, Jr., has so forcefully pressed us to understand and lament.[1] The critic can account for the meaning and function of the parts of a work only as they make up a whole; but the definition of the whole is required before the parts can be read in this way. This parts-and-whole curse is what, for the critic, dilutes the blessings of organic theory. We see only what our categories of vision permit us to see; and, having seen this way, we are reinforced in our prior vision by every detail, since each seems to support the theory of the whole that was required from the first for us to grasp the details as we have. In this manner, our every hypothesis about the total and partial meanings of a work is circularly self-enclosed. Thus insulated, the hypothesis is self-supporting—and utterly persuasive, even if sometimes its only victim is its creator.

Is this circularity of interpretive claims not really another guise for the circularity of value claims? Are the two not inevitably one at last? It is not far-fetched to suggest that the perspective that determines what we would have the work be in order to make sense of its parts is in its turn determined by our prior notion, implicit or explicit, of what we will value in poetry—or value as poetry. My essay has begun, and it will have to end, with this suggestion, so that I must deal with problems of interpretation and evaluation almost indiscriminately. The overlapping, if not the identity, of these circles would seem to make somewhat futile Hirsch's attempt—for the sake of an objective, scientific hermeneutics—to cut off interpretation from criticism. This is an attempt, incidentally, in which, despite enormous differences between them, Hirsch resembles Northrop Frye.

II

We recall, from the opening of the manifesto to the critical revo-

---

[1] His most extended treatment of the problem and its consequences is his *Validity in Interpretation* (New Haven, 1967), which includes, as an appendix, his influential essay, "Objective Interpretation," as it originally appeared in *PMLA*, LXXV (1960), 463–479.

lution he sponsored, the "Polemical Introduction" of his *Anatomy of Criticism* (1957), that Frye pleaded—in the tradition of our most serious critics of all ages—that we distinguish "inductive" criticism from the mere expression of taste and, consequently, make the developing structure of criticism crucially different from the history of taste. We must, he urges, avoid turning criticism into the stock-market fluctuations of literary fashion. The critic must not permit the incestuous interrelations between poet-function and critic-function which can at once over-value Donne in order to allow a necessary revolution in modern poetry and over-value certain modern poetic tendencies that reinforce the dominance of the school of Donne in questions of evaluation. Or substitute Blake or Hopkins, as the spirit or necessities of the moment move him, and the problem pointed out by Frye is the same.

I have myself been conceding the practical impossibility of keeping criticism inductive, of keeping taste out of it, once we first concede —in post-Kantian manner—the constitutive role of our categories of perception in conditioning all we experience. This is what is guaranteed by the hermeneutic circle and the consequent evaluative circle. However great our obligation as critics to distinguish what we see and how we value it from what is potentially there to be seen and what its value is, there is little point in denying the limits of our access. Who indeed can look on beauty bare? This is as much as can be said in defense of the modern critical habit—as I have described it—of blurring the lines between analysis and evaluation and blurring both with an *a priori* definition, necessarily reductive, of what poetry is, or had better be. I have acknowledged elsewhere the obvious presence of an *a priori* theory, implicit or explicit, consistent or inconsistent, coming between us and our experiencing (and, consequently, our valuing) the work before us, conditioning all we see and how we like it.[2] In light of these confessional concessions about the critic's burdens and his limitations, we may wonder how wishful Frye's thinking must be as he seeks to divorce criticism, as an objective discipline moving toward becoming a science, from both our subjective experiencing and our valuing of the object, two actions which he sees as interrelated and equally beyond the hope of being tamed by objective or inductive criteria.

Of course, Frye can save criticism from the subjectivity to which experience and evaluation are condemned only because he defines criticism as the systematic construct of a total hypothesis. For him it

---

[2] In "The Disciplines of Literary Criticism," *The Play and Place of Criticism* (Baltimore, 1967), especially pp. 142–146.

deals, not with the individual work as an entity, but with its share-holder's role in the total joint-stock enterprise which is all literature as the projection of the total human imagination. So for him the task of criticism is not the traditional one: it is to tell us, not what the work in its distinct singleness is and how we are to value it, but what its universalizing tentacles are that lead us outward to grasp other works and, with them, the total dream of man. Because criticism works only to establish this mythic *logos*, this system in its wholeness, it can hope for the scientific objectivity of its hypothetical total structure, having abandoned to untutored subjectivity the discreteness of our single aesthetic responses and their value. Those concerned with the more traditional roles of interpretation and criticism, as applied to single works, may wonder—once Frye's different use of the term "criticism" has been taken into account—whether any escape from the subjective has been achieved, indeed whether there has not been a retreat from the little that criticism (as normally defined) has accomplished in mitigating the egocentricity of our predicament. It is such termino-logical difficulties, perhaps, which have caused the endless disagree-ments about Frye's position on value.[3] Delicately poised as it is, this position can be seen as resembling Hirsch's only if we define it crudely and partially; it would take an essay as long as this one to begin to place it accurately.

Nevertheless, this position, however distorted through crude for-mulation, can be used to bring us again to the more open—if not totally dissimilar—proclamation by Hirsch of the desperate, long ignored need to separate the internality of interpretation from the externality of judgment. Unlike Frye, Hirsch has only the single liter-ary work—or, as he prefers to call it, the single text—as his object to be interpreted and valued. According to him, what we do with this text is properly called interpretation if we limit ourselves to the frame-work within which the author has willed or intended his creation. In this case we are concerned only with the text's "meaning." It is called criticism if we measure the text's relevance to whatever framework of our own we freely bring from the outside and choose to impose. But now we are dealing, not with the text's "meaning," but only with its

---

[3] See the essays and books referred to by John E. Grant in his "Checklist of Criticism of Frye's Work," in *Northrop Frye in Modern Criticism: Selected Papers from the English Institute*, ed. Murray Krieger (New York, 1966), espe-cially pp. 176–180. See also pp. 81–84 of that volume, from W. K. Wimsatt's "Northrop Frye: Criticism as Myth."

"significance." This is but another way of saying that as critics we are dealing, no longer with the work itself, intrinsically, in its own terms, but with our conceptual terms to which a partial and distorted abstraction from the work is adapted. It is the particular version of "metaphysical pathos" carried by each of us that predetermines and limits our criticism, the "significance" it finds. Any claim of value which we make necessarily refers the work, outside its own limits, to an alien criterion that may have to do more with us than with the work. How honestly can any of us altogether deny these charges?

The work itself, according to Hirsch, has been created in response to the demands of the mysterious entity he invents and terms its own "intrinsic genre" (not quite the work itself, since the work can be translated into it, yet as genre not broad enough to include any other work). It is this intrinsic genre that we as interpreters must find and use as our measure of the work. As soon as we have subjected the work to any other criterion, we impose upon it our own extrinsic genre and to this extent have violated the integrity of our (supposed) interpretive completeness, a completeness that should have been achieved by our establishing its intrinsic genre. We are to remember that this intrinsic genre has, for the author, been constitutive and not just heuristic. This is to say, it has become the formative principle in response to which the work has been created; it is not just our tentative invention of a helpful framework which never has been formulated as such or has functioned as an intrinsic control. For if this genre is merely heuristic, and not truly constitutive, then, no matter how close to the work itself it may be, the genre still is also an extrinsic genre only and enjoys no special privilege. Thus the intrinsic genre, as constitutive, has for Hirsch been a necessary theoretical invention to give interpretation a privileged, intrinsic status to which criticism can never be admitted. However, whether for the rest of us the intrinsic genre is more than a theoretical invention, whether any of us can see it as actually there—as not the work itself and yet so slightly broader that it comes tailored to suit only this work—all this is seriously questionable. The desire to free us from the contextualists' linguocentric trap, to allow a translation that still does not universalize, carries its own theoretical burdens of internal contradiction.

The invented entity, the intrinsic genre, may be as slightly useful, and as hazy, as that other invention used by Hirsch, the "intentional object." The "intentional object" is what the work phenomenologically becomes, out there beckoning to us in its singleness despite the chaos of our many varied "intentional acts." It remains out there where it has grown—a single, determinate entity—out of the author's intended or willed meaning. Such inventions—to which we may add that of a willed meaning—create what is for each or all of us inaccessible postulates as "mystical" as any of those in the recent critical tradition which Hirsch condescendingly rejects. We may suspect them of being a self-deceptive multiplication of merely verbal categories. And if we abandon the possibility of a constitutive intrinsic genre, with its strangely privileged status, then everything that we critics can make of the work or do to it is equally extrinsic and, finally, reducible to us and not it. We find no undistorted, neutral object to yield a neutral reading, no breathless object to precede our breathing upon it. Interpretation, then, must be thrown into the same pot as criticism, the one now seen to be as aprioristic as the other, as dependent upon the critic's projected categories. Once the author's constitutive genre is reduced to the interpreter's heuristic invention to grasp the ungraspable, the interpreter's language is fated to be distinct from the author's precisely as the critic's language is. The post-Kantian epistemology absorbs interpretation and criticism alike and leads to the blurring of their functions. Still, the critic-interpreter (I now join the two) must wrestle with these limitations, so that Hirsch's directions for help do satisfy our objective yearnings and may serve as guidelines permitting us to judge how appropriate to the object is each of the endless variety of aprioristic answers which recent criticism has arrogantly supplied.

We began by briefly examining the tradition after Richards and Eliot that led critics like Empson, Tate, and Brooks (it would not be hard to add others) to interpret the poem, to define it as poetry, and to honor it as a favored example of the art by means of a *priori*, theoretically derived characteristics. And we lamented the severe costs to our inductive hopes of this multiplicity of perspectives, even as we lamented more the inevitability of this procedure. As we look at other schools of critics, however, we are struck by extra-literary impositions far less attentive to any claims of what Hirsch calls "objective interpretation." After all, the efforts of contextualist critics, like the neo-Aristotelians we might call the genre critics, were initiated in large part out of their desire to return to the object, their subservience to their own metaphysical pathos notwithstanding. The hermeneutic circle may overlap the contextual circle of the work to an infinite variety of degrees, but it remains the critic's own circle. Still, when we observe what—in contrast to the contextualist or the neo-Aristotelian —the social-political commentator sees as the work, or what the historian of ideas or the biographical-psychological commentator or his recent apocalyptic descendant, the "vision" critic, sees as the work, we can appreciate the pragmatic value of these differences of degree even if theoretically, methodologically, we cannot establish any difference in kind among those circles that rotate around that crucial one the critic cannot penetrate.

Indeed, even out of Frye's "inductive" objectives, the myth critic can end by looking for, and valuing most, the work he can most readily tailor to his specifications, thus joining the others in the parade of most favored hypotheses and the most favored poems read to order to support them. All are busy in their own ways creating their structural models to characterize and reduce the manifold workings of the human imagination. Every critic might appear his own structuralist, with that recent arrival, the self-proclaimed structuralist, himself the archetype of the critic, who necessarily adapts the work to a model he claims to find immanently within it and who ends by substituting the model for the work. Geoffrey Hartman has performed a valuable service by placing Frye within the larger (and mainly Continental) structuralist movement as perhaps its most ambitious member.[4] Frye's continuing celebration of the creatures of imagination in their monumental configurations *is* a structuralist celebration. Like the structuralist, he must assume (as *his a priori* hypothesis of a total and coherent system) that structures in many sorts of discourse—literary and otherwise—are, in the end, open to similar analysis; are analogous, are through metaphorical transference related, and finally are potentially identical, as the analogous becomes the anagogic. Together as microcosm and macrocosm, they become the key to unlock the secret forming power of the human imagination. The critic thus projects a syntax —a generative grammar—of imagination upon the work which is made to match his structural model. Literature and other discourse are seen as the many versions of the Platonic Forms through which imagination, feeding itself and upon itself, grasps and creates its reality.

Though anti-formalist, Georges Poulet is finally not unrelated to this sort of structural monism. His phenomenological insistence always leads to the glorious identity of consciousness among reader, poet, work, the collapsing of the distinctnesses of time and space in the instantaneous union between every critic and poet-as-Mallarmé or Proust. And the most favored works, or the most favored readings which make most favored works, follow accordingly. In his structural

---

[4] In "Structuralism: The Anglo-American Adventure," Yale French Studies, XXXVI-XXXVII (1966), 148–168.

probings in the novel, René Girard ends by at once destroying all barriers, all mediation, between the vision of a character and his author, and creating a single—however dynamic—structural pattern which permits such instantaneity and identity to occur.[5] He thus seems to combine Poulet's phenomenology and structuralist method. And with so uniform a reading, concluding in his universal claim that, structurally and phenomenologically, all novels become the same novel, we indeed see this kind of criticism as providing an archetypal confession of the apriorism that Hirsch, for all his method, cannot purge from criticism conceived as a humanistic exercise.

III

Having confessed this much, how can the critic perform if he is to accommodate the myopia which plagues him? Let him first confront the obvious: The major difficulty in assigning value, that seems to dictate the total separation of evaluation from interpretation, is the fact that value cannot be a secondary quality, to borrow a term from an old-fashioned epistemology. As a tertiary or axiological quality only, goodness in art cannot be described as can the perceptible characteristics of the object about which interpretations can argue. Thus, in a way that would seem to lend comfort to Hirsch as well as Frye, value can be assigned to the cluster of features in the object we have described only by the intervention of a subject fiat: "let that be termed valuable which. . . ." And then follows the formula which fits those works which have the features we want. "The work is what I have been showing you it is. Well, that is how works ought to be, although I can hardly show you this claim in the same way." Thus the antique axiological problem: the critic cannot reduce value to fact without sacrificing ought-ness. But if the critic is to function helpfully as a critic of value, he must still manage to "anchor" the axiological to the observable features of that object, preserving its ought-ness only by the intervention of the subjective fiat, although he must hope to cover as many fellow-subjects—other readers—with it as he can. Which is to say, his requirements must come as close as he can make them to the limits of the object, provided we can agree about those limits.

The claim to value might rest tentatively on a hypothetical procedure that is admittedly tautologous: what can we require of a poem

---

[5] See *Deceit, Desire, and the Novel: Self and Other in Literary Structure*, trans. Yvonne Freccero (Baltimore, 1965), especially pp. 293–310.

if it is to function most effectively as what it is; if, that is, it is to per-
suade us to a peculiarly poetic response? At this point we could distinguish, analytically and heuristically, among kinds of response—say, to
use the usual Kantian triad, the cognitive, the moral, and the poetic
(or, more generically, the aesthetic).[6] I call these distinctions analytic
and heuristic because our purposes require us to define them, in
advance of actual experiences, in their pure states even though the
actual experience of the most pristine of us is very likely a messy com-
posite of them. I am not interested in whether they occur as defined
or in whether, if they did, that would be a good thing; only in what
they would be like if they did, so that we can characterize what objects
would be like that were constructed to lead us toward one or another
of them.[7] It would not be difficult to find the distinguishing characteristic of aesthetic experience, in contrast to the others, to lie in its
self-sufficiency, what Eliseo Vivas calls its "intransitive" quality. From
the experience so defined, it would be even less difficult to move to
describe the characteristics of an object that would be expressly constructed so as to facilitate that experience, to lead us toward it, provided we were willing to lay at rest our normal cognitive and moral
propensities to go through objects rather than to be contained by
them.

About several points let me make explicit the modesty of these
claims. First, I am suggesting nothing about the value of the poetic
or aesthetic experience. It is postulated only as a possible psychological datum, to be described as having certain characteristics, degrees
of attentiveness, disinterestedness, and the like. Secondly, I am not
suggesting that only certain kinds of works can produce this experience in us. As a psychological fact, it will occur when it occurs, and
the control of it by the stimulating object cannot be predicted. Nor,
thirdly, can I say the experience is better when it can be referred to
and anchored in an object. But when it is, we can point to its cause

---

[6] Here and in what follows I am clearly indebted to the analysis made in
many places by Eliseo Vivas. See especially his "The Artistic Transaction,"
The Artistic Transaction and Essays on Theory of Literature (Columbus, 1963),
pp. 3–93. He would add the religious experience to those I have named, but
since my interest here is to furnish a brief exposition rather than to argue
whether there are three or four varieties, I stick with the more conventional
distinctions of Kant.

[7] Vivas, on the other hand, insists on the empirical basis of these definitions. See his complaint against my concessions, *The Artistic Transaction*, pp.
201–202n.

and expect that it can be repeated with different subjects. So I can say, once we have agreed about the defining qualities of this experience as an *a priori*, analytic type, that certain objects can be seen and described as being so constructed as to produce it in us, provided we are willing, and knowledgeable enough, to submit. Every aspect of the work would contribute to keeping us enclosed within its symbolic world, preventing our escape to the world of reference and action beyond, the world of external relations in which the cognitive and / or the moral tend to preclude the merely aesthetic. We can see how criteria like irony, ambiguity, paradox, tension are given value as means of preventing that escape. From this enclosure of internal relations, at once mutually inhibiting and mutually satisfying, can arise such a series of criteria according to which we can judge the work's efficacy as an *aesthetic* object, that is (to return to the tautology), one whose nature and purpose seem calculated to lead us toward the experience we have denominated aesthetic. But we predicate the nature of the experience only to get us toward certain kinds of characteristics in the object, characteristics that, by remaking language, transform its signs into weighty, substantive, corporeal symbols.

Is this an assertion of its value? Only if we return to the hypothetical statement with which we began. *If* we wish to consider the work only in terms of an aesthetic function (though there may be others, perhaps better ones), *if*, that is, we wish to have a work perform what literary discourse is uniquely able to perform, then we can speak about how successfully or unsuccessfully it performs such a function. Of course, this does not reduce tertiary to secondary qualities, value characteristics to descriptive ones. For we have really decided no value questions. It may, after all, be more valuable not to consider a work this way, so that what we have determined may very well be what Albert Hofstadter has termed aesthetic validity rather than aesthetic value.[8] Nevertheless, it is enough to let the critic proceed: his circular theoretical assumptions permit him to define what the poem *qua* poem, having a unique and indispensable function, must do insofar as he, as *literary* critic judging its literary (and thus aesthetic) quality, can speak authoritatively about the relative quality of its performance. What he sees and how he judges follow accordingly.

---

[8] "Validity versus Value: an Essay in Philosophical Aesthetics," *Journal of Philosophy*, LIX (1962), 607–617. See Monroe C. Beardsley's response, "Beauty and Aesthetic Value," pp. 617–628.

Obviously, this is how the contextualist critic has proceeded. We can define his methodological limitations and, from these, his own metaphysical pathos from which his vision, almost on its own, ensues. The predisposition about closed form dictates that all "literary openness" be automatically excluded from his realm of value (or validity). Whatever he relegates to allegory he excludes, as a crypto-rhetoric, from the honorific realm of poetry. Whatever he attributes to the intrusion of unformed experience, he charges with aesthetic illegitimacy in the service of that chaotic rebel, the anti-poem. For him either case leads away from the peculiar response that poetry alone can arouse. No detraction from its value, mind, but, within the qualifications of that "if" clause, with which we saw him begin, the unenclosed work cannot be admitted. Similarly, we can see, in his predisposition toward the unique contextual system of meanings, in his distrust for normal language in its universal dimensions, an affinity for the unique dynamics, the existential immediacy of particularized experience, an experience that betrays contradictory elements beyond rational reconciliation. Even so formalistic a doctrine rests on thematic presuppositions, on what has been called metaphysical pathos. How, then, is this critic to deny the partiality of his vision and his judgment, the intrusion upon these of his role as twentieth-century man? But which of us can claim more or deny less, for all the barrage of objective procedures he lays down? The humanist is always embarrassed by his parochialism and restless within it, if too honest to deny it.

IV

So we grant that our hermeneutic methods are, as methods, pretty frustrating and, as a would-be science, not very promising. Nevertheless, we must not, through mistaken analogies, look for methods of establishing the meaning of texts as positive as those used to establish the texts themselves. For, as we have seen, texts and the meaning of texts do not at all have the same availability to us. We see with Hirsch the inevitability of the hermeneutic circle. From this the sad fact follows that the reader of criticism can only move from one argument-from-coherence to another, choosing among the several self-enclosed, self-justifying, self-convincing interpretations poised against each other but not speaking to each other, shut off in their several universes of discourse. Or is this too extreme? Can they really never speak? Can critical discourse really become as insulated as the fully functioning poetic system? But let us provisionally accept as

much, reserving our qualifications until we have explored the consequences of so extreme a notion.

The only way to escape the hopeless movement among alternatives as pictured by Hirsch is to search with him for the intrinsic
genre, at once outside the work and encircling it. This search carries
Hirsch outside the hermeneutic circles of so-called "intrinsic" meanings for the "extrinsic" evidence that can help us to narrow the range
of probabilities within which our interpretation should occur. For we
must move toward the author's intended or willed meaning and can
use all the help we can find. We can, Hirsch suggests, move beyond
alternative circles toward the more probable interpretation only if we
continually narrow the genre that guides our vision of the work and
defines how it is to take its meaning; but only by resorting to materials
that can establish horizons, boundary limits, to all that our competing
critical imaginations can claim to discover within the inner workings
of the piece. The generic is the typical so that, as Hirsch demonstrates
in his attempt to decide between Bateson and Brooks on Wordsworth's "A slumber did my spirit seal," the interpreter should invoke
the "typical" Wordsworth to establish the bound or narrow the genre
within which one reading is the more probable. With admirable can-
dor Hirsch insists that he has given us a method to establish not correct readings, merely more probable ones. But, he persists, if interpretation is to grow as a rational procedure, then—as more exact
sciences have learned—probability is as much as we can hope for.

But perhaps it is not in literary criticism as Aristotle says it is in
tragic literature, that a probable impossibility is to be preferred to a
possible improbability, although to acknowledge this much is to
forego our hopes for criticism as a progressive science. After these past
decades of intensely pondering over the special intricacies of the syntax of poetic discourse, we have learned, perhaps more than anything
else, that our greatest works achieve that status largely by their defiance—through transformation—of what we might predict as being
typical or probable from all the extrinsic data we can summon. And
the critic had better not surrender his rare chance to be correct in
describing the work's miraculous movements just in order to be faithful to a notion of a "more probable" hypothesis. Is it better to support
a "science" that would make so rare a chance non-existent? The great
work, in its workings, its transformations, may very well demand the
less probable, if not the least probable, hypothesis, if we were to judge
from all that we could know before the work or outside the work.
Hirsch continually maintains the Aristotelian truism that we must
limit our methods by the capacities of our subject, that we must

expect no more precision than the nature of our subject-matter permits. But since he does *not* see poetry as a specially empowering and empowered form of discourse, with systematic interrelations among its elements—language, character, scene—that allow its escape from the limited functions of other discourse, he need not yield up his general method for interpreting *all* texts (poetic and otherwise) by way of more probable rather than less probable hypotheses. For if poetry has as discourse no different ontological status, no other way of meaning, it can have no exemption claimed for it.

This, however, is to shut off an entire range of possibilities that recent criticism has tried to keep open. Hirsch can claim rightly that to deny in poetry the rights of the more probable hypothesis (the degree of probability depending on our ability to circumvent the circle by imposing evidence from the outside that can narrow the work's "intrinsic genre") is to deny any chance for positive knowledge in criticism, the knowledge of our probability of being right. But we must ask again whether, in poetry of the first rank, Hirsch's "intrinsic genre" is constitutive rather than merely heuristic. It may very well be so in non-poetry and in poetry not of the first rank, which must lean on (and open outward to) organizations of meaning beyond itself. But surely it is begging the question to begin by assuming that it is necessarily so in poetry of the first rank as well, so that this poetry is denied the power to create its meanings anew, out of its own system. Our empirical sense should warn us against this question-begging after all we have learned from recent criticism of these unpredictable powers of poetic discourse. The failures and excesses of this criticism need not lead us to insist that a science of criticism can be substituted for it, and its successes may rather lead us to believe that to assert the possibility of a science of criticism may indeed be to beg the question, so long as that would-be science depended upon a probability count determined by a constitutive intrinsic genre imposed from outside. Nevertheless, as the alternative from inside, we must grant Hirsch, only rival hypotheses, supported by data created by a vision each hypothesis allows, can throw the hard edges of their circles against one another.

What is the good, Hirsch laments, of limiting interpretations to what the text can adequately sustain, when—thanks to the hermeneutic circle—our ingenuity can force the text to sustain an unlimited number of *self*-sustaining, mutually incompatible interpretations? But has our experience not shown that the text does not, with equal adequacy, sustain all comers? that, in fact, the experienced reader can discriminate among all but a few through the failure of most of them to account for crucial features of the text? Hirsch would grant as much, properly being concerned by the rival claims of those few and our powerlessness to adjudicate with authority among them. We must all share this concern, although our anxiety to find a way to adjudicate must not lead us to adjudicate on the wrong grounds, to feel a security which our decision—and our way of reaching it—cannot support.[9]

The recalcitrant (or retrograde?) denials of Hirsch's claims may very well deny the interpreter his chance at *positive* knowledge, the knowledge of our *probability* of being right. But what (we must answer by asking) if this very service to the rational probability of being correct often makes the interpretation in fact wrong? And what if the frequency of being wrong increases with the value of the work at hand? Would that not alter what is probable when it comes to that strange miracle, the fully functioning poem? The critic, then, if he must choose between the probability of being correct (via methods true of discourse generally) and actually being correct (though unable to know it or argue for it since it is an improbable correctness), must of course choose the latter or else desert his subject for another subject, one more conveniently dealt with. He would have to insist on a higher (and, on some grounds, an improbable) probability for poetry, though one attained by methods that are essentially non-transferable. At issue, of course, is whether or not the usual sort of probability tests, on which progress in textual interpretation normally depends, work with the sort of discourse that our best works become. Nor can we, after invoking with Hirsch the Aristotelian injunction about matching methods and objectives to their subjects, begin by indiscriminately reducing all texts to the sort of text with which general probability-

---

[9] We can, for example, share Hirsch's impatience with the mistaken student reading he cites of Donne's "A Valediction Forbidding Mourning": that it concerns an impending death rather than a more temporary separation of the lovers. Still he does spend disproportionate time on several occasions in *Validity in Interpretation* fearing the possible failure of internal evidence and invoking other sorts of evidence. Yet he admits the strength of our case, for the more modest reading can come from the poem before we turn for support to Donne's other valediction poems and to his general metaphorical habits. One metaphor after the other and the tone of the whole can be marshalled to demonstrate the temporary and even almost trivial separation rather than the deathbed separation seen by melodramatic students too romantically prepared—even if such students will not respond to the persuasiveness of such ample evidence. But, of course, no critic with critic friends wiser than himself can deny that there are cases far more difficult—if not impossible—to resolve.

testing can deal. Hirsch so reduces them by making no distinctions among texts and thus conceding to the literary text no difference that would exempt it from the general method.

If verbal meaning were individual and not a type, it would not be knowable, Hirsch confesses in his final Appendix. Therefore, he argues, let us by all means always keep it a type. If, unlike other meanings, poetic meanings should turn out to be individual, as contextualists have insisted, then Hirsch would have to maintain that we must not confound meaning itself, which like the Kantian thing-in-itself would remain unknowable, with our hypotheses about meaning, which can be rationally debated and judged. His sensible claim is that we can make progress only by attending what can be rationally debated and judged (whence the imposition of types). My own notion is that, confronted by the mysteries of a meaning that may not permit us to know it, we must choose either to bend our language and methods in order to grope after it, however imperfectly, catch as catch can, or to sit pristinely back, purifying our language and methods, in hopes that this purification is relevant and that this language and these methods may after all lead toward that elusive meaning. I clearly lean toward the sloppiness of the first of these alternatives, Hirsch toward the increased precision of the second. I allow the meaning to remain individual and hence even ultimately elusive; and I believe even Hirsch's evidence would lead in this direction, were he not so anxious not to preclude positive knowledge and its necessary methods. For me it is once more the old joke about the man who tried to find his precious lost object by looking for it, not where he lost it, but where he found the light to be brightest. The joke arises because he should have been looking for the object rather than for the light, however convenient the latter. I am suggesting that we stay in the murky area close to the meaning which is our object, that we avoid light for light's sake, the clear well-lighted methods and language that may after all be the wrong light, or light wrongly located, in view of what we must try—painfully, even perhaps futilely—to uncover.

On his side Hirsch could claim—and persuasively—that I am introducing an anti-rational mystification, that I am begging the question in my own way since I deny to his methodical procedure any access to our best works by declaring them out of bounds by *fiat*. It is so: my claim can break out of its own circle only by appealing to that common experience that assures us that the poetic system does work in ways that exempt it from our general classification of texts. With a method that disdains any scientific ambition, I can say no more than the special nature of the work's workings permits me to say: that the critic—trapped in the aesthetic object in its aesthetic function—does better to trap himself in his hermeneutic circle and, without resorting to those externally imposed boundary limits that may distort the work, to rely only on the clumsy give-and-take of the Socratic method to make his dubious progress toward satisfactory interpretation. He can do no more than throw his own self-enclosed circle against all comers in hopes of seeming more adequate to his data. On some rare occasions he may even change someone's mind or be persuaded to change his own. There will, as Hirsch would insist at once, be dismal impasses between mutually incompatible hypotheses, each persuasively self-enforced. But we must live with these, struggling—sometimes helplessly—between them, confident that it is not less necessary to do so here than in all other areas (most of them other-than-literary) of our profoundest verbal and substantive disagreements with our fellows. And we shall be truer to our data—our finest literary works—if we persist thus unprogressively in our retrograde circles rather than surrender their defiance of whatever external predictabilities and probabilities may be imposed in order to move toward the certainty that resolves contradictions. After all, this is the stubborn way our strongest criticism has always—and not altogether unsuccessfully—proceeded. It is questionable whether we can legislate a way of doing better.

Through this defense of intra-systematic, circular interpretation, my own (by now self-conscious) smuggling in of value notions has been hardly concealed. What else can I have been doing in my constant suggestion that the usefulness of Hirsch's method is inversely proportionate to the work's literary value—the better the work the less its nature permits it to succumb? The resistance to external appeals, the need to trace and retrace internal circularities—these become testimony to the work's aesthetic success. Convince us that external horizons are adequate as well as relevant, that the circle is *not* closed, and critics like me downgrade the work as poetry. Indeed we begin to withdraw that honored title, poetry, from the work and become ready to consider it as something else. For value remains embedded in our aprioristic definitions, as it has been shown to be for critics in this tradition from the start of this essay.

So criticism thus practiced is not to be a science, not even having enough method to separate matters of value from matters of fact. I follow this commonplace, that criticism is not a science, with the self-righteous assertion that it ought not to be, Hirsch (and, though less strenuously, Northrop Frye) to the contrary notwithstanding. Does not even Hirsch, who ends by looking in the poem by Wordsworth for evidence of that Wordsworthian typicality which he must assume before beginning, demonstrate that his broadening of method finally only broadens the range of his own circularity? Hence the further commonplace that criticism is but an art, a highly—and necessarily—imperfect art, a half-art. We must not, even theoretically, expect too much of it, though neither must we, out of our disappointments caused by its confusions with mere taste, surrender its intimate connections to the realm of value. Nor surrender the primacy of the critic's imaginative power, his constitutive power at once to project and perceive (or, more precisely, to perceive by projecting) interpretation and value. As critics we must always expect and hope for the perfection of the work of art. Perfection of the work itself, yes; but of criticism—especially as it includes judgment—never!

V

I have argued similarly in a recent book that criticism, though it may freely play, must remember its place. This was meant to be a humbling reminder of its unscientific and only half-artistic nature. Each critical performance, provided its object is a *proper poem* (defined in the questionable, aprioristic way I have outlined), is a struggle and compromise between the untranslatable symbolic structure that is the poem and the more commonplace symbols brought to it by the critic. These symbols define and limit his vision. Thus it is that each critical performance is also a struggle and compromise between the new vision of the unique work and the old vision of its reader which seeks only to reinforce itself. There is the apparently paradoxical double activity which (1) permits the self-conscious reader (really another term for the critic) to grasp the work only by way of the categories of vision he brings to it—which is to say, only by reducing the work to what his prior self will permit it to be—and yet (2) leads him to broaden what his vision has been in order to accommodate the newness in the work. In the latter case his limited view has become less limited, his old view renewed, literally reconstituted into something more comprehensive, freshened by immediacy into a reshaped definition. If he engages only in the first half of this double activity—if he only uses the work for visionary reinforcement, accommodating it to his generic vision that pre-exists it—then of course he has denied literature and our traffic with it its proper function of making him more than—or different from—what he was, of educating him into *its* mode of vision. Why bother opening ourselves to the great imaginative works if we foreclose their impact?

On the other hand, if the work as we perceive it is, in post-Kantian terms, defined by the visionary categories through which we constitute it, how can it reconstitute those categories? How can any element outside our categories, from the nakedly existing work itself, intervene to transform those categories, rendering their pre-existing versions obsolete?

Clearly the personal fact of what literary works do for us and the historical fact of what they have done for their cultures point to an inescapable phenomenological fact, of interest to Hirsch as well as to me: Though the work seems to exist for us only as our categories permit it to be defined, only as our commonplace, generic symbols reduce and distort its unique symbolic structure—still there must be something in the work as it must exist (or subsist?), on its own, outside our categorical structures and symbols. This something can force our structures and symbols to work radical transformations upon themselves, in response to their own commands, as it were, though prompted from beyond their autonomous realm. What more persuasive indication can we have that there is a something out there, beckoning us, soliciting our wilful subjugation to its power to change our ways of seeing and of living? The control imposed by its objective, reconstituting force upon our subjective, constitutive powers challenges the limiting and distorting projections of our categories, finally breaking through the self-sufficient insulation of our visionary circles. What a Shakespeare or a Melville can do to the metaphysical and moral shapings of our imaginations, a Mallarmé or a Proust can do to our consciousness of space and time as he freezes our world or lets it flow.

Whatever our decision about the ontological status of the literary object, its existence, meaning, and value before we collide with it, we know that we can speak of it only out of the dust of that collision. We pick ourselves up, no longer quite the same selves, and try to speak with precision about what has struck us and the force of its impact. And we probably will give the usual one-sided version of what has transpired and what sort of antagonist we have encountered. Who is to correct us except others who have suffered similar encounters and whose descriptions will be as partial and as self-serving? None may deny the encounter, none deny how profoundly he has been changed by it; yet each will have his own version, each levy his own assessment. Since each is changed, the alienating quality of the force —and its forcefulness—are beyond question. There should be a way of getting at the force itself by comparing versions and visions—a way of subtracting what each was from what he has become and finding some critical range among the differences. It is an inexact and inconclusive way, though perhaps the only way we have. For there is no way of getting at the force—despite radical disagreements about its nature—except through our radically diverse, autonomous experiences of it, even as our judgment of these experiences must be modified through dialogue. Our depositions attesting to the independent existence of the force, its neutral objectivity as *ding-an-sich*, are useless to us so long as we are not permitted to get at it in its independence and neutrality. Those of us whose impatience leads them to introduce systematically controlled, firmly generic criteria from the outside in order to eliminate the subjective angle of vision are deceiving themselves about the positive nature of the results they look for. The force which is the work itself lives only in those singular visions and in their mutual modifications by men honestly trying to look, and to move, beyond their own limitations, though it is these limitations that define who they are. Yet it is the force that helps define who they are to become.

University of California, Irvine

ON VALUE JUDGMENTS

Northrop Frye

I should warn you at once that I have nothing new to say on this question, nor can I discuss it on Mr. Krieger's level. I must bring it down to the context of our own professional routine, and though I might rationalize this context as being existential, committed, and the like, even here all I can offer is an analogy that seems to me pedagogically instructive. The pursuit of values in criticism is like the pursuit of happiness in the American Constitution: one may have some sympathy with the stated aim, but one deplores the grammar. One cannot pursue happiness, because happiness is not a possible goal of activity: it is rather an emotional reaction to activity, a feeling we get from pursuing something else. The more genuine that something else is, the greater the chance of happiness: the more energetically we pursue happiness, the sooner we arrive at frustration. The more one says he is happy, the more quickly we get out of his way to prevent him from making us miserable.

So with the sense of value in the study of literature. One cannot pursue that study with the object of arriving at value judgments, because the only possible goal of study is knowledge. The sense of value is an individual, unpredictable, variable, incommunicable, indemonstrable, and mainly intuitive reaction to knowledge. In knowledge the context of the work of literature is literature; in value judgment, the context of the work of literature is the reader's experience. When knowledge is limited, the sense of value is naive; when knowledge improves, the sense of value improves too, but it must wait upon knowledge for its improvement. When two value judgments conflict, nothing can resolve the conflict except greater knowledge.

The sense of value develops out of the struggle with one's cultural environment, and consists largely of getting an instinct for the different conventions of verbal expression. All verbal expression is conventionalized, but we quickly realize that some conventions are more acceptable to the social group we are associated with than others. In some societies, including our own until quite recent times, the different conventions were linked to different social classes, and high and low speech were at least symbolic of the conventions of lord and peasant respectively. Today we still have, despite the linguists, distinctions between standard and substandard speech, and a corresponding distinction, though one quite different in its application, between standard and substandard writing. The critic who fights his way through to some kind of intuitive feeling for what literary conventions are accepted in his society becomes a representative of the good taste of his age.

Thus value judgments carry with them, as part of their penumbra, so to speak, a sense of social acceptance. One of the first papers I heard at an MLA conference was a paper on Yeats by W. H. Auden, given at Detroit in 1947. He referred to Yeats's spiritualism in terms of its social overtones of lower-middle class credulity and drawn blinds in dingy suburban streets, and remarked that A. E. Housman's Stoicism, while it may have been no less nonsense, was at any rate nonsense that a gentleman could believe. There was of course an intentional touch of parody here, but actually Auden was putting an evaluating criticism into its proper, and its only proper, context. Every attempt to exalt taste over knowledge has behind it the feeling that the possessor of taste is certainly a gentleman, while the possessor of knowledge may be only a pedant.

The task of the evaluating critics, who review contemporary books and plays, is partly to prevent us from trying to read all the books or see all the plays. Their work is quite distinct from that of the literary scholar who is trying to organize our knowledge of our past culture, even though it is called by the same name and engaged in by many of the same people. The literary scholar has nothing to do with sifting out what it will be less rewarding to experience. He has value judgments of selectivity, just as any scholar in any field would have, but his canons of greater and less importance are related to the conditions of his specific research, not directly to the literary qualities of his material.

There is a vague notion that historical criticism is a scholarly establishment, and that all critical methods which are not simply branches of historical study, whether explicatory or archetypal, are anti-historical, and ought to be applauded or denounced as such. But, of course, every great writer who lived in a different time or cultural orbit from ourselves is a challenge to the assumptions on which our evaluative statements are made, and knowledge of his assumptions makes our own more flexible. The fundamental critical act, I have said elsewhere, is the act of recognition, seeing what is there, as distinct from merely seeing a Narcissus mirror of our own experience and social and moral prejudice. Recognition includes a good many things, including commentary and interpretation. It may be said—in fact it has been said by Mr. Krieger, and said very well—that it is not really possible to draw a line between interpretation and evaluation, and that the latter will always remain in criticism as a part of the general messiness of the human situation. This may often be true as regards the individual critic. Nevertheless there is a boundary line which in the course of time inexorably separates interpreting from evaluating. When a critic interprets, he is talking about his poet; when he evaluates, he is talking about himself, or, at most, about himself as a representative of his age.

Every age, left to itself, is incredibly narrow in its cultural range, and the critic, unless he is a greater genius than the world has yet seen, shares that narrowness in proportion to his confidence in his taste. Suppose we were to read something like this in an essay published, say, in the eighteen-twenties: "In reading Shakespeare we often feel how lofty and genuine are the touches of nature by which he refines our perceptions of the heroic and virtuous, and yet how ignobly he condescends to the grovelling passions of the lowest among his audience. We are particularly struck with this in reading the excellent edition by Doctor Bowdler, which for the first time has enabled us to distinguish what is immortal in our great poet from what the taste of his time compelled him to acquiesce in." End of false quote. We should see at once that that was not a statement about Shakespeare, but a statement about the anxieties of the eighteen-twenties.

Now let us suppose that an evaluating critic of our own age goes to work on Dickens. He will discover that melodrama, sentimentality, and humor bulk very large in Dickens. He feels that a critic of our time can accept the humor, but that the melodrama and sentimentality are an embarrassment. He has to pretend that melodrama and sentimentality are not as important as they seem, or that Dickens has a vitality which carries him along in spite of them. He will also realize that his own age sets a high value on irony, and dis-approves of coincidence or manipulated happy endings in plots and of exaggerated purity in characters. So he will bring out everything in Dickens, real or fancied, that is darkly and ambiguously ironic, or hostile to Victorian social standards, and the coincidences and the pure heroines and the rest of it will be passed over—in short, bowd-lerized. To interpret Dickens is first of all to accept Dickens's own terms as the conditions of the study: to evaluate Dickens is to set up our own terms, producing a hideous caricature of Dickens which soon becomes a most revealing and accurate caricature of ourselves, and of the anxieties of the nineteen-sixties.

As long as criticize means evaluate, the answer to the question: "Whom does the critic criticize?" seems at first a very easy one. The person the critic criticizes is, of course, the poet, whom the critic, in the traditional metaphor, judges. The drama critic attends a play and then writes a review judging it; if he is a literary scholar, then he reads the great poets in order to judge them too. Who would bother to be a critic unless one could be in the position of judging the great-est poets of the past? Alas, this carryover from judging to studying does not work, and the literary scholar, many bitter and frustrating years later, discovers that he is not judging the great poets at all. They judge him: every aspect of past culture shows up his ignorance, his blind spots, his provinciality, and his naiveté. When criticize means evaluate, the answer to the question "Whom does the critic criticize?" turns out to be, in scholarship, the critic himself. The only value judgment which is consistently and invariably useful to the scholarly critic is the judgment that his own writings, like the morals of a whore, are no better than they should be.

Of course literature, as an object of study, is a limitless reservoir of potential values. Think of how largely American nineteenth-century writers bulk in our cultural imaginations today, and of how impov-erished those imaginations would be if they did not include such fig-ures as Ethan Brand or Billy Budd or Huckleberry Finn. Yet it is not so long ago that the question was frequently and seriously asked: "What on earth could you find to say about American literature?" There is in fact nothing in past literature that cannot become a source of imaginative illumination. One would say that few subjects could be duller or less rewarding than the handbooks studied by Miss Frances Yates in The Art of Memory, yet her study has all the mental exhilaration of the discovery of a fine new poet. But when value is totally generalized in this way, it becomes a superfluous conception.

Or rather, it is changed into the principle that there is value in the study of literature, which is an unobjectionable way of stating the relationship.

The experience of literature is not criticism, just as religious experience is not theology, and mental experience not psychology. In the experience of literature a great many things are felt, and can be said, which have no functional role to play in criticism. A student of literature may be aware of many things that he need not say as a critic, such as the fact that the poem he is discussing is a good poem. If he does say so, the statement forms part of his own personal rhetoric, and may be legitimate enough in that context. Naturally a reader of a work of criticism likes to feel that his author is a man of taste too, that he enjoys literature and is capable of the same kind of sensitivity and expertise that we demand from a good reviewer. But a writer's value-sense can never be logically a part of a critical discussion: it can only be psychologically and rhetorically related to that discussion. The value-sense is, as the phenomenological people say, pre-predicative.

The study of literature, then, produces a sense of the values of that study incidentally. The attempt to make criticism either begin or end in value judgments turns the subject wrong side out, and the frequency of these attempts accounts for the fact that more nonsense is written in literary criticism, especially on matters of theory, than in any other scholarly discipline, not excluding education. Fortunately, its practice is considerably better than its theory, even when its practice includes MLA papers and doctoral theses on the birthday odes of Colley Cibber. No one deplores more than I do the purblind perspectives of scholarly critics, or the fact that so much criticism is produced with so little intellectual energy that it has all to be done over again. Still, it is better not to adopt a critical approach which makes the writing of sense impossible, however lugubrious the result of better premises may often be. With the enormous increase of personnel required in the humanities, I foresee a time when demands that every scholar be productive may be reversed into efforts at scholarly contraception. This may lead to a growing awareness of the difference between the criticism which expands our understanding of literature and the criticism which merely reflects and repeats it.

In the meantime, the effort to reverse the critical machinery continues to be made, usually in some such terms as these: Is not a value judgment implied in, say, choosing Chaucer rather than Lydgate for an undergraduate course? Surely if we were to elaborate a theory explaining why some writer is of the first magnitude, and another only of the tenth, we should be doing something far more significant than just carefully studying them both, because we should also be proving that it was less important to study the smaller man. I do not know of anybody who claims that a valid theory of this sort exists, but I have often been reproached for not devoting my energies to trying to work one out. The argument reminds one a little of that of Sir Thomas Browne that a theory of final causes, working through universal principles of design like the quincunx, would give us a master key to all the sciences.

It is also part of the great Northwest-Passage fallacy of criticism which always gets stuck in the ice of tautology. The greatest writers are—let me see—imaginative rather than fanciful, or possessed of high seriousness, or illustrative of the sharpest possible tension between id and superego. The critic invariably discovers these qualities in the writers he considers best, overlooking the fact that they are merely synonyms for his preferences. The circumambulation of this prickly pear can go on for centuries, as long as the terms used are brought up to date in each generation. Or one may draw up a list of categories that appeal to the sensibilities of the critic because they are fashionable in his age, and call them characteristic of all great literature of all periods. The effect of this is to canonize the taste of that age, and make it into a dogma binding on future generations. I. A. Richards made a parenthetical suggestion about such universal categories in Practical Criticism, but obviously soon realized, not only that the procedure involved was a circular one, but that, once again, such phrases as the "inexplicable oddity" of birth and death merely echoed the anxieties of the nineteen-twenties. For those who wish to persist with this or similar methods, a certain degree of paranoia will be found most helpful, if not essential.

It is because I believe in the value of literary scholarship that I doubt that value judgments have a genuine function in acquiring it. Those who try to subordinate knowledge to value judgments are similarly led, with a similar consistency, to doubt that genuine knowledge of literature is possible, or, if possible, desirable. There are many ways of expressing this doubt, or disapproval. One is the chorus that has for its refrain: "But literature is alive, and you're anatomizing a corpse." Such metaphors take us back to the vitalism that has long since disappeared from biology, and the scholarly critic is constantly being told that he is leaving out whatever the objector regards as the seat of the author's soul, whether his heart, his blood, his guts, or his testicles. The basis of this response is a fixation derived from adolescence, when the sense of social approval is so highly developed, and when it seems so utterly obvious that the end of reading is to assimilate everything into the two great dialectical categories of value judgment, which in my own adolescence were "swell" and "lousy." But it seems to me (if we must use these metaphors) that there is only one thing that can "kill" literature, and that is the stock response. The attempt of genuine criticism is to bring literature to "life" by annihilating stock responses, which of course are always value judgments, and regularly confuse literature with life.

On the next level there is the notion that university deans and chairmen demand a certain amount of historical research from new recruits as part of a kind of hazing process, before one is allowed to start on one's proper evaluating work. This research is assumed to exist all on one level, and to be nearly exhausted, so that one is now forced to look for something like the Latin exercise books of Thomas Flatman or the washing bills of Shackerley Marmion. The appearance of every genuine work of literary scholarship knocks the bottom out of this notion, but it revives in each generation of graduate students. More sophisticated versions of the rejection of knowledge are, first, the helpless historical relativism which says that as Samuel Johnson or Coleridge made some of the mistakes likely to be made in their day, so we can only go on making a fresh set of mistakes, and can learn nothing from our predecessors. Second is the assumption that most interpretation, if at all subtle or difficult, is something that the author could not have understood, and hence has simply been imposed on him by the critic, a pretext for an activity begun in self-hypnosis and sustained by group hysteria. If anyone doubts that such a reaction exists, he has probably never written a book on Blake's Prophecies.

In short, the more consistently one conceives of criticism as the pursuit of values, the more firmly one becomes attached to that great sect of anti-intellectualism. At present it seems to be fashionable to take an aggressive stand in the undergraduate classroom, and demand to know what, after all, we are really trying to teach. It appears that we are concerned, as teachers, with the uniqueness of human beings, or with the fullness of humanity, or with the freedom to be aware, or with life itself, or with the committed ironies of consciousness, or with learning to be at home in the world, or in fact with anything at all, so long as it sounds vaguely impressive and is not reducible to treating literature as something to be taught and studied like anything else. Seek ye first the shadow, we are urged, and the mere substance will be added unto you, if for some reason you should want it. It seems to be in literature that the teacher is most strongly tempted to cooperate with the student's innate resistance to the learning process, make himself into an opaque substitute for his subject instead of a transparent medium of it, and thereby develop his charisma, which is Greek for ham. But as values cannot be demonstrated, the possession of them is realized only by their possessors, hence the more evangelical the sales pitch, the more esoteric the product. I would of course not deny that teaching is a different activity from scholarship, and that many assertions of value are relevant to the classroom that are not relevant to the learned journal. But I think that in literature, as in other subjects, the best students are those who respond to intellectual honesty, who distrust the high priori road, and who sense that there may be some connection between limited claims and unlimited rewards.

University of Toronto

LITERARY EVALUATION
AS KNOWLEDGE

E. D. Hirsch, Jr.

Descriptive and normative judgments have ever been intertwined in criticism and literary theory. (The same is true of most intellectual activities, including mathematics.) Historically, this state of affairs has raised two separate questions in literary theory: (1) On what grounds is it true to say that value is an essential property of literature, and that valuation is therefore an essential element of description? (2) What, if any, are the normative criteria which, when applied to literature, will yield not only definitive evaluations but also accurate descriptions? Although the second question has consumed much theoretical energy in the recent past, I believe it is true that no judicial criteria can yield either definitive evaluations or accurate descriptions. It is well, therefore, to keep the questions separate.[1] In this paper I shall be concerned with the first question; it has been receiving renewed attention, as the papers by Mr. Krieger and Mr. Frye in this collection attest. The contribution I shall try to make to the discussion is a technical one in which I shall be recalling some pertinent observations of Immanuel Kant.

The main point at issue between Mr. Frye and Mr. Krieger is the long-standing controversy between the separatists and the anti-separatists—between those who wish to separate the serious study of literature from mere ideology or taste, and those who find the attempt undesirable or philosophically naive. Most contemporary critics have taken a stand, if only implicitly, on one side or the other, and on this point Mr. Krieger is right to place me in the school of Frye. Yet

---

[1] A detailed account of my reasons for denying privileged status to any criteria of literary evaluation will appear in the forthcoming *Yearbook of Comparative Criticism.*

the position of Mr. Krieger and the anti-separatists is, I believe, sound with respect to some aspects of the problem, and in this essay I shall be particularly concerned to explore those aspects. I hope that the exercise will help diminish disagreement over the issue.

The goal of Mr. Frye and the separatists is to isolate literary study from the vagaries of changing tastes so that, purged of these variable elements, the descriptive side of criticism will come into relief. Literary study will then take its proper place among the progressive disciplines of learning; it will aspire to the condition of science. In his "Polemical Introduction" Frye had the courage to speak of a "scientific element in criticism" and the rhetorical wisdom to caution "readers for whom the word 'scientific' conveys emotional tones of unimaginative barbarism [that] they may substitute 'systematic' or 'progressive' instead."[2] Although Frye mistakenly equated "scientific" with an all-encompassing scheme of classification instead of with a critical testing of hypotheses, that did not diminish the force of his demand that literary description be purged of arbitrary evaluation. For if the ups and downs of the literary stock exchange are integral to literary study, then farewell progress, farewell genuine knowledge.

The anti-separatists, on the other side, have answered that all criticism, including Frye's, is larded with value judgments and that no one should want to divorce description from valuation: "What is the point of a fugitive and cloistered study which, under the pretext of scientism, disregards the very knowledge that is peculiarly appropriate to literature? The undertaking would signal a regression into that literary positivism and pseudoscientific methodology against which the whole modern movement in literary scholarship has rightly rebelled. If the price of system and progress in the humanities is the exclusion of everything peculiarly humane, then the price is not worth paying. In any case, the alternatives are not so grim as that. Genuine knowledge of literature is possible, and it necessarily includes knowledge of values."

So much for metaphysical pathos. The question whether value judgments must adhere to the description of literature is not in itself solved by taking sides on the relative desirability of different critical procedures. Both sides have stated the problem as a theoretical issue, and it is a problem that is amenable to theoretical solution: Value judgments must adhere to literary description if, and only if, literature possesses ineluctable value as part of its essence. The theoretical argu-

---

[2] *Anatomy of Criticism* (Princeton, 1957), pp. 7–8.

ment against separatism is therefore stated cogently and in its proper terms by René Wellek:

> We cannot comprehend and analyze any work of art without reference to values. The very fact that I recognize a certain structure as "a work of art" implies a judgment of value. The error of pure phenomenology is in the assumption that such a dissociation is possible, that values are superimposed on structure, "inhere" on or in structures.[3]

Any accurate descriptions of literary works must therefore have reference to the values that make them literature and not another thing. And description of value is evaluation; to separate the two is an ontological impossibility. Wellek is very explicit: we cannot even *comprehend* a work of art as in itself it really is without at the same time making a judgment of value. This assertion is worth wrestling with at the most serious level, and seriousness requires one to ask first what "value" in such a context means or ought to mean.

The word "value" is sometimes used as if it represented an independent reality like a rock or a piece of gold. Yet nobody has ever seen or imagined a value as an independent reality. Something that "has value" must be actually or potentially worth something to somebody in some respect; outside of that relationship, it cannot have that value. No doubt some things are valuable in certain respects to human beings generally, but this hardly bestows on us the right to speak of such value relationships in absolute terms.

> While Man exclaims "See all things for my use!"
> "See man for mine" replies a pamper'd goose.

Value as such, absolute value, would be value-to-God, and even in this ultimate, presumptuous judgment the concept would still be relational and specific: valuable to God in what respects? The words "value" and "valuable" considered apart from such relationships correspond to nothing that exists or could exist. This view is often called an "instrumentalist" conception of value, and, while I prefer the adjective "relational" to "instrumental," I accept it as being the only conception which, in my knowledge of the subject, corresponds to reality. That the conception is perfectly adequate for dealing with

---

[3] René Wellek and Austin Warren, *Theory of Literature*, 3rd ed. (New York, 1956), p. 156.

aesthetic and other values found in literature has been argued convincingly by Monroe Beardsley.[4]

Yet despite this caveat, which would lead to some modifications in Wellek's phrasing, I believe he is right to say that a literary work "is a totality of values which do not adhere to the structure but constitute its very nature. All attempts to drain value from literature have failed and will fail because its very essence is value."[5] An instrumentalist would, of course, want to ask Wellek how literary value (which must reside in the relationships between a work and its readers) could at the same time constitute the work's "very essence." The hardheaded instrumentalist position would seem to require a qualification of Wellek's claim, since for an instrumentalist *nothing* could have value as part of its essence. Yet I believe that the two views are reconcilable, and, moreover, that the process of reconciling them will solve one of the knottier problems of critical theory.

The problem is essentially the one which Kant confronted in his *Critique of Judgment*. The crucially important element in Kant's theory for the issue at hand is not his definition of aesthetic value, but rather his argument for the objectivity of such value. For Kant as for Wellek, value is conceived as belonging to the very essence of a work of art:

If one declares something to be beautiful . . . he judges not solely for himself, but for everyone, and then speaks of beauty as if it were a property of things. Hence he says the *thing* is beautiful.[6]

The aesthetic value of anything cannot be dissociated from the thing itself as an object of aesthetic contemplation. Thus, Kant ends the *Analytic of the Beautiful* with the sentence: "The beautiful is that which is recognized without concepts to be the object of a *necessary* delight." For the anti-separatists everything depends upon whether this position can be successfully upheld. If so, it must follow that no description of literature can properly escape judgments of value, since Kant's argument about beauty would apply to all the values

---

[4] See especially his essay "Beauty and Aesthetic Value," *Journal of Philosophy*, LIX (1962), 617–628.

[5] *Concepts of Criticism*, ed. Stephen G. Nichols, Jr. (New Haven, 1963), p. 52.

[6] *Critique of Judgment*, Section 7. Quotations from this work, cited by section, are based on (but do not in every case precisely follow) the excellent new translation by Walter Cerf, ed., *Analytic of the Beautiful*, The Library of Liberal Arts (Indianapolis, 1963).

which belong to the work as a necessary property of its being perceived.

· Kant is properly solicitous to preserve the relational character of beauty even while he argues for its ineluctability, thereby meeting the requirement that any value, including that of beauty, must be relational. A beautiful object is inherently beautiful because it is or ought to be universally beautiful *to* mankind. For the experience of beauty is subjective; its "objectivity" consists in the universality of the subjective experience:

Such universality is not an objective, but only a subjective quantity of judgment . . . a subjective universal validity. . . . Precisely for this reason, the aesthetic universality ascribed to a judgment must be of a special kind. For it does not connect the predicate of beauty with the concept of the object in its entire logical sphere, yet nevertheless extends it over the whole sphere of judging subjects. (#8)

This concept of a necessary and therefore universal subjective judgment of value has been a stumbling block to modern readers of Kant, for whom the differences of subjective values among men have seemed more noticeable than the similarities. Everything we have learned since the great historicist revolution which gathered force in Kant's lifetime has confined us in our scepticism towards the idea of a common human nature. Yet Kant is quite explicit in stating that some such idea is required to uphold the theory of necessary value: "Only under the presupposition of a common sense does it become possible to make a necessary judgment of value."[7] As a modern writer, Mr. Wellek, naturally enough, eschews this exigency by speaking of values as though they had independent objectivity instead of subjective universality, but for an instrumentalist, Kant's position must be considered the right one. The crucial point is that the observable variations in our subjective value judgments do not affect Kant's profound argument in defense of "objective" values. For he openly concedes that individual tastes are variable:

Violet is a soft and lovely color to one person, cold and dead to another. One man loves the sound of wind instruments, another that of strings. It would be folly to quarrel over such matters and to condemn judgments differing from ours as incorrect. (#7)

---

[7] Section 20. Thus Kant: "Nur unter Voraussetzung, sage ich, eines solchen Gemeinsinns kann das Geschmacksurteil gefällt werden." *Kritik der Urteilskraft,* ed. K. Vorländer (Leipzig, 1924).

To grant this much from the start, Kant must have in view some very powerful arguments for a common sense among mankind and the necessary value judgments it entails. If his arguments hold (and I believe that they do), then Wellek's insistence on the inseparability of literary description and evaluation must be correct.

The easiest and most direct way to defend the concept of necessary value would be to argue that a poem or other work of art cannot be perceived (in Wellek's phrase "comprehended") except as an object of value. The value of the work would then be part of the cognition itself. Yet this direct line of argument is vulnerable, since the necessary value to us of something we perceive (its beauty to us, for example) can be realized only *after* we have perceived it. If we try to make a value judgment before having cognized the object, the best we can say is: "This experience is giving me pleasure," but we could not impute a universal validity to the value judgment, since it would not be grounded in something universally shareable, namely the cognition of the work. Early in the *Analytic* Kant devotes a long section to the question whether a judgment of value "is prior to or posterior to cognizing the object," commenting that "the solution to this problem is the key to the critique of taste" (#9). His answer is straightforward:

Nothing can be universally communicated and shared except cognition and representation in so far as it belongs to cognition. For only in so far as it belongs to cognition is representation objective and has a universal point of reference with which everyone's faculty of representation is obliged to tally. (#9)

Kant's insistence on the priority of cognition is therefore a logical inference about the relationship of cognition to necessary judgments of value; it is not an empirical description of psychic events. Within this limitation the argument is compelling.

It is not yet clear, however, why Kant should have considered this point the key to the critique of taste, particularly since his defense of necessary value judgments must depend not on the priority of cognition but on the existence of a universal common sense. The two issues turn out to be intimately connected. Behind his formidable facade Kant is often a great ironist and a great dramatist of ideas. He has carefully erected all the major obstacles to his goal in order to show that the obstacles themselves will become the high road to his conclusions. He has conceded that judgments of beauty are subjective: further, that necessary subjective judgments require a universally shared object of cognition and a universally shared subjectivity (common sense). Yet he has also conceded that subjective value preferences are highly variable. The *peripeteia* and *anagnorisis* of this intellectual drama occur at the end of the *Analytic* when Kant proves that *a common sense is required not merely for a universal subjective judgment but also for a cognition of the object itself.* That is why the priority of cognition is the key not only to the critique of taste but also to the problem addressed in this essay. Kant has provided, I believe, the only possible grounds for asserting the inseparability of literary description and value judgment, and is quite justified in maintaining that his solution is "worthy of the greatest attention" (#9).

His argument is in many ways analogous to that of the first *Critique*. There one of his goals had been to defend the objectivity of scientific knowledge, just as here he defends the objectivity of aesthetic judgment, but in this case, instead of being forced back to the most abstract and primary categories of experience, he is stopped short in a domain which requires the application of cultural categories to the facts of cultural experience. Kant's procedure shows very clearly that it was he and not the twentieth-century phenomenologists who first conceived the value-laden objects of cultural experience as epistemological ultimates. It was he, not ourselves, who first discovered the irreducible connection of "fact" and "value" in the *Lebenswelt*. For Kant argues that the objects of cultural experience, no less than those of primary sensation, are constituted by the mental organization of the perceiver. "The eye altering alters all." The object of cognition, when we perceive a flower, a poem, a painting is in itself constituted by the "mental set" we adopt to perceive it. If we are to have a shared cultural object of cognition, we must also have a "common sense" with respect to that object.

Thus, at the end of the *Analytic* Kant rests his case for inherently necessary value judgments on the fact that our very cognition of a shared cultural object presupposes a shared system of feelings and attitudes with respect to it:

If cognitions must be able to be shared, then that mental state in which the cognitive powers are attuned for cognition must also be able to be shared. And in particular that proportion or ratio of the cognitive powers that is required to turn a representation (by which an object is given us) into knowledge must be able to be shared. For this ratio [i.e., "mental set"] is the subjective condition of knowing, and without it knowledge as an effect could not arise. (#21)

Kant's subject being the judgment of beauty, he defines the mental set narrowly as "a harmony of the mental powers," but his argument holds by implication for any other sort of value judgment. This should be kept in mind in following the next stage of his argument when he connects a shared cognition not only to a shared mental set but also, necessarily, to a shared feeling:

> There must be one harmony in which the inner ratio is most propitious to the quickening of mental powers for the purpose of cognition, and this harmony can be discovered in no other way than by feeling. . . . Now this harmony itself must be able to be universally shared [otherwise the object could not be] and consequently also the feeling of it on the occasion of a given representation. (#21)

To deny this chain of reasoning would be equivalent to denying the possibility of any sort of knowledge:

> It follows that there is a good reason for assuming a common sense. And we can do so without resting our case on psychological observations. Rather, we assume a common sense as the necessary condition without which knowledge could not be shared universally; and this is a possibility that is presupposed in every logic and every principle of knowledge that is not sceptical. (#21)

By refusing to separate value preferences from the mental set required in certain types of cognition, Kant has made it impossible to separate value judgments from the cognition of art. His refusal seems to me altogether valid. For example, the degree to which some element in a poem receives emphasis in our experience of it will be partly determinant of its structure for us, partly determinant of what it *is* in our cognition of it. At the same time, the imposition of emphasis implies a judgment about relative importance—importance to us as well as to the poem since the poem for us is our cognition of it. But the judgment of relative importance is entirely an adjunct of the mental set adopted in a particular cognition, and is inseparable from the feeling which accompanies that particular kind of importance.

Kant's stress on feeling in subjective value judgments is thus eminently justified, and is a welcome antidote to the circumspectness with which nowadays we invoke vague, hypostatized entities called "values." Modern linguists and literary theorists do, of course, speak of "affective meanings" in contradistinction to "cognitive meanings." But how these two kinds of meanings relate to one another, or how indeed there could be such an entity as an affective *meaning* has not so far been satisfactorily explained.[8] Kant solves the problem by showing why cognitive meaning (the only kind there could be) is in most utterances accompanied by necessary affects in our cognition of it. The correlation of cognition and mental set makes this inevitable, and completely obviates the need for recourse to such a mysterious entity as affective meaning. Moreover, the correlation of cognition and necessary affect in experiencing literature is very much a part of what we mean in speaking of "literary values." For in addition to whatever social and ethical value literature may have, much of its special value to us must be of the kind which carries "subjective universal validity" and is inseparable from feeling.

The implications, however, of this necessary union between "fact" and "value" in literature cannot be altogether congenial to the anti-separatist position as it is usually formulated. The Kantian argument does not support a necessary union of description and evaluation as those terms are usually understood. When Kant's argument is translated into terms specifically appropriate to verbal works of art it becomes an argument for the inseparability of *meaning* and value, and it takes the following form: The meaning of a literary work can be cognized only by adopting the specific mental set which is constitutive of that meaning. In relation to that mental set, the meaning will necessarily be accompanied by specific subjective value judgments. Since the relationship between the meaning and the subjective attitudes which constitute it is ineluctable, so therefore is the relationship between the meaning and the universal subjective value judgments which it sponsors. For example, we might read the following as a somewhat resentful accusation:

> Thou, silent form, dost tease us out of thought
> As doth eternity: Cold Pastoral!

If so, the meaning of the lines must be associated with a momentary diminishment of our exalted admiration for the Grecian urn and the consolation it brings. If, on the other hand, the words "tease" and "cold" are understood not as correlative to an attitude of resentment, but rather to a sense of still greater exaltation which transcends "all breathing human passion," then the feeling of admiration is not

---

[8] For a recent discussion and account of previous work on "affective meaning" see John Parry, *The Psychology of Human Communication* (London, 1967), pp. 65–69, 212–217.

diminished or qualified but accentuated. Or, to suggest still another possibility, the words "tease" and "cold" might carry meanings correlative to more complex feelings, negative in some respects, emphatically positive in others. In each of these cases, *the cognitive meanings of the words would be just as different as their correlative affects.* And, more to the point, the different meanings could have existence only through the different constitutive mental sets which sponsored both the meanings and their correspondent affects.

This brings us to a problem which Kant omitted to consider. Which of the various possible meanings attachable to Keats's lines is the one which carries "universal subjective validity" and therefore necessary value? One correct answer would be that each of these meanings carries its own necessary value, but this answer does not satisfy the requirement set by Kant and Wellek that the value be judged "as a property of the thing," not of one individual's perception of the thing. "Universal subjective validity" requires that the correctness (universal shareability) of the cognition be established, not just the correlation between cognition and value. Kant passes over this problem with the observation that "there must be one harmony in which this inner ratio is the most propitious to the mutual quickening of the mental powers for the purpose of cognition" (#21). In other words, Kant's criterion for the correct cognition of a beautiful thing is that under it the thing becomes the most beautiful, the harmonious quickening of the mental powers the greatest. But, obviously, this criterion will serve only so long as beauty is the value being sought. If the most beautiful meaning (in Kant's sense) happens not to be the meaning intended by the author (as it would not be in, say, one of Tolstoy's late stories), then the problem of arbitrariness arises. The whole ground of "necessary value" would be destroyed, since the necessity rests entirely on a shared object of cognition. "Only in so far as it belongs to cognition is representation objective and has a universal point of reference with which everyone's faculty of representation is obliged to tally" (#9).

It could be argued, of course, that the shared object of cognition (Tolstoy's story) is the same for everyone who adopts the aesthetic mental set defined by Kant. But even as an imaginative exercise this procedure would not carry the universal imperative originally demanded, since the aesthetic stance would not be "the one most propitious" to a cognition of Tolstoy's meanings. An implicit conflict would persist between Tolstoy's meanings and the ones realized by a purely aesthetic mode of contemplation. This is a crucial weakness in Kant's argument. With a work of art, the only object of cognition having implicit claim to be "a universal point of reference" is the shareable object cognized by its maker. The claim of privilege for any other object would be too arbitrary to carry genuine universality. The only values which can be considered intrinsic properties of a work of art are those which attach by subjective necessity to a re-cognition of the author's work.

This conclusion is altogether consistent with Wellek's assertion that "we cannot comprehend and analyze any work of art without reference to values." It also causes us to recognize a distinction between the different kinds of value judgment present in literary commentary. Some are intrinsic and necessary; some are not. The values which adhere by necessity to a description of meaning are those which subsist between the meaning and the subjective attitudes which constitute it. In other words, the only unavoidable judgments of value in literary commentary are those which are necessarily implied in interpretation. An interpretation of meaning cannot eschew the value judgments which are correlative to meaning; one cannot perform an ontological impossibility. On the other hand, it is quite possible to eschew other kinds of value judgment in literary commentary, although one should not avoid responsibility by doing so. I shall conclude this essay by showing that these other kinds of value judgment have as much inherent claim to genuine knowledge as the necessary value judgments implicit in interpretation.

The only universally valid cognition of a work of art is that which is constituted by the kind of subjective stance adopted in its creation. The value judgments correlative to that kind of mental set are thereby given in the very act of cognition. But other attitudes towards the work are obviously possible, both on the part of the critic and on the part of the author himself when critically judging his own work. On the surface this would seem to raise a problem for the Kantian schema, since the work can have existence only through the subjective stance which constitutes it; to interpret it from another stance would be to cognize another, different work. But this is not necessarily what happens. The judicial critic and the self-critical author can judge the work from an alien stance without relinquishing the privileged subjective stance which constitutes the work's meaning. A ready example of this simultaneous empathy and alienation is found in our experience of drama. In *Oedipus Rex* we understand from Oedipus' own point of view what he says about ridding Thebes of its plague, and at the same time we *judge* what he says from a quite different standpoint. It would be inaccurate to say that we interpret Oedipus' words differently from the way he meant them; the effect of Sophocles' irony depends upon our interpreting Oedipus' words precisely as he meant them and at the same time passing a judgment upon that meaning. Irony, whether verbal or dramatic, always entails this simultaneous adoption of two different mental sets, neither stance being assimilated to the other.

I choose an example from drama rather than from another form because in drama, even for purposes of pure interpretation, we must entertain at least two standpoints: that of the character who speaks and that of the playwright who (unbeknownst to the character) is controlling the significance of what he says. In principle there is no reason why this encompassing of one subjective stance by another could not continue indefinitely—the character's meaning judged and encompassed by that of the playwright, and both of these judged and encompassed by a critic. (I recently read an essay criticizing a critique of Johnson's criticism of Shakespeare's comedies.) The crucial point is that the application of an alien subjective stance does not necessarily destroy or distort the subjective stance which constitutes the meaning of a work. The integrity of the work with its attendant values can be preserved while judgment is passed upon it. Indeed, if this primordial integrity is not preserved, a critical judgment could not be valid, since the object criticized could no longer be "a universal point of reference with which everyone's faculty of representation is obliged to tally."

The example of drama points to another characteristic of literary evaluation which is crucial to its status as a form of knowledge. Nearly everyone would agree that the playwright's implicit judgment upon the speeches of his characters is an essential part of a play's meaning. But if this kind of critical judgment is granted an objective status in our knowledge of literature, there is no inherent reason why a critic's judgment of the *playwright's* work should not in turn be granted a similarly objective status. To qualify as objective knowledge, judicial evaluation need fulfill only two criteria: (1) that it be a judgment about the work and not about a distorted version of it, and (2) that the judgment be accurate with respect to the criteria applied. When Plato judges that Priam's appeal to Achilles is bad literature because it encourages men to act in an undignified manner, his judgment is correct on that criterion if (and only if) that is indeed the effect which Homer's description has. If a critic announces that literary excellence resides in the perfect correlation of a work's style with the ethos of the age when it was written, then any work which has this quality will also have literary excellence—on that criterion. Judgments that are accurately made upon explicit criteria furnish the grounds of their own validation and therefore qualify as knowledge. Of course, arguments about the relative merits of the various judicial criteria in literary criticism are another matter. These arguments cannot be resolved absolutely, but only with reference to further criteria (about which the disputants may or may not agree) regarding the proper functions of literature and criticism. It nevertheless remains true that accurate judicial evaluations made under explicitly chosen criteria have as much objectivity as accurate interpretations.

This analysis has led, therefore, to the following conclusions:

1. The interpretation (description) of a literary work is necessarily correlative to the particular subjective stances which constitute its meanings.

2. Affects and value judgments necessarily subsist in the relationship between meanings and these correlative subjective stances. These value judgments are therefore inherent in literary description.

3. Judicial criticism encompasses this unity of meaning, stance, and value by an alien (sometimes hostile) stance which can nevertheless preserve the integrity of the primordial one.

4. From this alien standpoint, new judgments of value and significance can be predicated which are just as objective as pure description.

Finally, I should like to add a fifth conclusion which has been implicit throughout the analysis. The ascription of inherent value to a literary work of art is made possible by Kant's insight into the necessary subjective component that constitutes any shared cultural object. So far as I am aware, this Kantian insight provides the *only* grounds for ascribing necessary value to a literary work of art. Yet Kant's principle by no means limits itself to literature or works of art in general. If it holds at all it must hold for any cultural object whatever, and emphatically for any use of language. A technical essay, an ordinary conversation, or a poem has, therefore, necessary, inherent values; of course, the values are different, but the structure of the argument for their existence is the same. It follows that there is no sound reason for isolating literature and art in a mysterious ontic realm apart from other cultural realities. The inherent values of literature are not thereby protected, but called into question by being made the objects of a mystique. Humane studies are best served by welcoming, not deploring the fact that the values of literature are continuous with all other shared values of human culture.

University of Virginia

A MODEST PROPOSAL FOR CRITICS

Wayne Shumaker

The practice of standing back now and then from what one has been doing, as a painter steps away from his canvas to see it in deeper perspective, cannot do much harm and may do considerable good. It is, I think, especially valuable for the literary critic, whose proper subject matter has no hard edges but merges almost indistinguishably with literary biography, history of several kinds, sociology, psychology, and linguistics. The context of every piece of criticism further includes general aesthetics, the intellectual discipline which determines what aspects of the literary object are responsible for its status as art; and this despite the fact that aesthetic standards may be undeclared and perhaps unconscious. In what follows I propose to assess the present state of criticism, at first favorably, later not. I acknowledge gladly, however, having learned much from the very critics—most of whom will remain unnamed—against whose practices I shall demur in the hope of showing that some of our present critical orthodoxies need reexamination.

I begin on a note of celebration: in many ways criticism is better than it has ever been. As our general knowledge increases we see more deeply into nearly everything, literature included. The number of people engaged in intellectual activities is enormously larger than in the past, communications are more efficient, and, not least important, we have learned to take empirical data seriously. In consequence, we wonder at and revere such critics as Aristotle and Samuel Johnson without feeling that we must share their principles. For our own critical techniques we go to our contemporaries—rightly, as the modern physician does not use a stone knife for surgery. I do not deny that earlier critics were larger, and in some ways wiser, men than we are.

The scientific genius of Archimedes may have been greater than that of Galileo, or that of Galen greater than that of Pasteur. But we must start where we are and cannot allow admiration or a nostalgia for bygone simplicities to draw us into accepting archaic notions.

A few examples will illustrate. When Johnson protests against the dramatic unities, we assent and are grateful:

It is false, that any representation is mistaken for reality; that any dramatick fable in its materiality was ever credible, or, for a single moment, was ever credited. . . . He that can take the stage at one time for the palace of the *Ptolemies*, may take it in half an hour for the promontory of *Actium*.

A comment like this represents a permanent conquest of common sense over mistaken Authority. Much in Johnson's criticism, however, has only historical interest. "A poet overlooks the casual distinction of country and condition, as a painter, satisfied with the figure, neglects the drapery." *Does* the painter always neglect dress? The answer is obviously no. *Ought* he always to neglect it? Not if the dress interests him as much as, or more than, the face. In a novel, similarly, the background may be more fully rendered than the personages. Who am I, or who was Johnson, to tell an artist what is most interesting about his subject? The fully articulated train of reasoning by which Johnson would have supported his generalization would have included assumptions we need not accept.

Aristotle poses harder problems; and indeed the *Poetics* is perhaps the most impressive critical document ever written, as well as certainly the most influential. Much in it has lasting relevance; but again we must discriminate. When Aristotle wrote that "Tragedy endeavors, as far as possible, to confine itself to a single revolution of the sun, or but slightly to exceed this limit," he was evidently making an induction about Greek tragedy which so far as I know is sound. When he says that unity of plot does not consist in the unity of the hero, or that of all plots the episodic are the worst, or that the bringing of a villain to justice is not tragic, he appears to speak plain sense. Actually these arguments are self-contained because definitional. The *Poetics* is full, however, of *obiter dicta* which, despite their intelligence in the immediate context, have no bearing on essential tragedy, if such a thing exists: "Every tragedy, therefore, must have six parts, which parts determine its quality—namely, plot, character, diction, thought, spectacle, song"; "There is a type of manly valor; but valor in a woman, or unscrupulous cleverness, is inappropriate"; and much else of the same kind. Nobody would now condemn a tragedy because it lacked song, and Greek drama itself, in such figures as Medea, Antigone, and Clytemnestra, did not lack brave and clever women. Aristotle's neat categories—tragedies required choruses, valor belonged properly to men—did not derive wholly either from observation or from logical necessity but from his philosophical method, which involved sorting things out into convenient pigeonholes on the basis of prominent characteristics.

So far there may be little disagreement; but I expect resistance when I add that the central critical doctrines of the *Poetics*, brilliantly suggestive as they are, serve chiefly as points of departure for argument. The theory that tragedy provides an outlet for stored-up emotions of pity and fear is no more plausible than a current view that the protagonist is a scapegoat through whom the spectator's vices and errors are punished so that he can be reintegrated with the community, and Aristotle's insistence that the victim be a man of high estate is less useful, in our democratic age, than the opposite one that a Willy Loman or a Schill (in *Death of a Salesman* and Dürrenmatt's *The Visit*) is a proper hero because he resembles the common spectator. Indeed, such an academic exercise as a paper on "An Aristotelian Analysis of Webster's *The Duchess of Malfi*" calls less for critical insight than for ingenuity—like, for instance, a paper on whether Milton would have supported the Vietnamese War—and is unwise because it implies the permanence of Aristotle's criteria. If the typical modern critic has less sheer intellectual power than Aristotle, he is far more sensitive to differences and has a much stronger sense of contingency.

The same comparative judgment can be rendered of premodern analyses of literary detail. The decay of rhetorical study is sometimes lamented on the ground that modern criticism has been deprived of traditional analytic concepts; and indeed the traditional names of "figures of speech and of thought" are useful descriptive counters. Aside from praising figurative language as serving to add dignity or ornamentation to discourse, however, the older use of the terms was chiefly in exhaustive lists which offered short examples torn out of context. The actual working of literary details in their settings was fully specified only in wild allegorical interpretations of the kind attempted by Natalis Comes and Henry Reynolds (in the *Mythomystes*). Nowhere in premodern criticism do I know of so detailed and sensitive an explication as the following, taken from an essay by a young critic who has so far achieved no special recognition:

The working of the simile of Hercules [in *Paradise Regained*, IV, 560–571] itself expresses this double relationship of contrast and fulfilment between the heroic tradition and Christ. The struggle with "Earth's Son" aptly typifies the strenuous aspiration of ideal heroism; moreover, "Jove's Alcides" may well suggest the Son of God, and even without any such suggestion the reader would surely be predisposed to look for a correspondence between the exemplary hero and Christ. This correspondence seems immediately to conflict with the action on which the simile is constructed, for it is Satan who plays Hercules' part of lifting his antagonist high in the air in order to destroy him at last; but no sooner does that apparent contradiction appear than it is triumphantly resolved. The strenuous aspiration of the pagan hero is suddenly revealed as vain, Satanic pride; yet in the same instant its apparent opposite, Christ's still obedience, is revealed as the true fulfilment of the heroic type. The expectation that Hercules would correspond to Christ is fulfilled mysteriously.[1]

The critical techniques which allow such penetration are now so commonly available that college undergraduates can express perceptions which no premodern critic would have known how to formulate (and therefore could not have attained).

In contrast, the peaks of earlier practical criticism are chiefly memorable exclamations: Dryden's appreciation of Chaucer, "Here is God's plenty," Sidney's acknowledgment that an old ballad moved him like a trumpet, Ben Jonson's generous admission that his rival Shakespeare was the delight and wonder of the stage. Persistent digging into literature, which brings out into public view its sinews and even, at times, its corpuscles, is modern. Except in editing—for example, Bishop Newton's admirable 1749 edition of Milton—earlier practical criticism is doctrinaire or impressionistic. Even the bad modern critic has ready at hand sharply honed critical instruments unknown to his most gifted forerunners.

So far I have praised—I hope ungrudgingly, and certainly, so far as I can know my own motives, honestly. The past is behind us; we cannot hope to recapture it, and probably, in spite of its superficial attractiveness, it was worse than the still unsatisfactory present. To understand the past as well as we can is a part of wisdom; to accept from it what has enduring value is both wise and moral; but not to recognize that in many ways we have passed beyond it is stupid. Except for the limited purpose of understanding an author's

---

[1] John Coolidge, "Great Things and Small: The Virgilian Progression," *Comparative Literature*, XVII (Winter 1965), 22.

intention more sympathetically, criticizing on the basis of a pre-nineteenth-century aesthetic would be like trying to drive a Roman chariot or an Enlightenment carriage on a modern freeway. Nevertheless we should strive to make the present as good as we can; so I proceed to offer suggestions.

In order to begin very gently, I quote a sentence which is absolutely unexceptionable as to fact and judgment: "After the first period of poetry had reached its climax with the two great funeral elegies, *Lycidas* and *Epitaphium Damonis*, Milton started making plans for poetry in the major genres—perhaps part of the meaning of the 'fresh woods and pastures new' at the end of *Lycidas*." The author of this passage enjoys deserved repute, and I believe him also to be an estimable human being. Yet the sentence contains what I believe to be an error of tact and implies, very faintly, a questionable doctrine.

The error of tact is debatable, but I mention it because doing so permits me to approach the whole area of critic-reader relationship. The book from which the sentence is drawn is addressed to "relatively inexperienced students" who do not, presumably, already have a firm grasp of the chronology and content of Milton's writings and therefore might have appreciated a cleaner separation of facts from critical inferences. Early in my teaching career I learned that a student who read (for example), "When, tentatively on September 22, 1862, and permanently on January 1, 1863, Lincoln issued an Emancipation Proclamation freeing the slaves, little immediate change in their situation resulted," would remember the failure of the Proclamation to have much effect and would forget immediately—if he ever noticed—the dates of its issuance. The Miltonic critic I have quoted is not ignorant of hard factual data, but by example he encourages his audience to form the habit of dropping facts rather airily into their own papers and to put primary emphasis on their intellection. The likely result, which of course is not produced by one such sentence but by thousands, heard from a number of teachers and read in a preponderant majority (perhaps) of the critics whom they are led to believe admirable, is a prizing of brilliance over knowledge. Criticism thus tends to become a rather showy activity which attracts students who think themselves exceptionally bright and are inclined to aim—whether they realize it or not—rather at being impressive than at discovering critical truth.

The judgment of the sentence would be petty were it not suggested by the method and tonality of the whole book. Sometimes the generalities stand utterly without factual or logical support. At times a cooperating reader who is also well informed can supply the support himself. When the author asserts that "The supremacy of Adam over Eve is the free and human relation," we can understand him to mean that Eve voluntarily submits herself to Adam and that the relationship is peculiarly human because only human beings have free will. When, however, he declares with utter self-assurance that "A bullying or dictatorial attitude toward one's wife would be merely one more example of what Milton calls man's effeminate slackness," the natural reaction is to ask why. Perhaps the author thinks that such an attitude is endemic rather to women than to men. Again, and slightly more probably, he may have reflected that weak men may conceal their lack of masculinity by blustering. Since he does not tell us, however, we cannot be sure; and in the meantime we may decide that the husband's attitude could better be called presumptuous. The mystification reaches down into the exposition. "There remains," we are told at one point, "of course only the fourth question." Of course; the author's confidence inclines us to assent. But what were the other three? Perhaps I am especially obtuse, but after a search I was able to find only two. We are not, however, expected to be made uneasy by the lack of clarity, and in the end we may gather, ungraciously, that we should trust the writer because he knows himself to be more intelligent than his readers or has been granted a special revelation.

The impression would, I am sure, be mistaken. The writer I have quoted is authentically intelligent, authentically well informed, authentically perceptive. I write of tone and method, not of the man; and in other critics these are exaggerated. From some criticism one would gather that the author wears gold-encrusted vestments as, in a tone of calm superiority, he pronounces judgments from an elevated *cathedra* to lesser mortals who can be saved by faith; or else, more rarely, his bearded lips mutter oracular truths while from beneath shaggy brows his eyes flash with unspoiled intelligence. In either case he demands assent not because what he says can be shown to make sense but because it is he who has spoken. No doubt this sort of thing is more common in the worst sort of graduate papers than in published criticism; but we have all read both journalistic and academic criticism which seems aimed at producing a subservient acquiescence. At the absolute nadir is criticism which appears to have been written for no other purpose than to allow the author to scintillate. With that we need not presently be concerned, for I take it that in real criticism a literary subject is central. But we all yearn for recognition, and just now we may feel that in an age of science we apostles of literature are insufficiently credited with wisdom. The effect is partly the limitation of criticism to a coterie, with an accompanying loss in cultural significance, and partly the convincing of university students—especially, perhaps, those who most need some acquaintance with it—that literature is not their cup of tea. Although I cannot inveigh against self-importance without revealing myself to be drawn to it—we all hate most hotly in others the faults we recognize in ourselves—I urge that we eschew the grand manner in criticism both by avoiding an authoritarian tone and by supporting every statement we make by evidence or reasoning, as the context may require.

The hieratic attitude (I abandon the Unspoiled Sage, the Academic Hippie) derives, I suspect, from a mistaken view of what literature itself is and the kind of knowledge it contains; and this consideration is more fundamental. (I come at last to the doctrinal error mentioned earlier.) From some of the writings of Allen Tate and John Crowe Ransom one gathers the impression that literature contains the highest knowledge accessible to men and that Newton or Boyle or Kant had only a modicum of the intellectuality of a respectable poet. Eliot's poetry, which by implication lays claim to all knowledge worth having, makes the reader who does not have freshly in mind all the literature to which it alludes feel inferior; and Pound seems to believe that only a poet can have sound economic views. Even Empson (for whom I feel irritated admiration), by finding multiple meanings in every phrase he examines, convinces us temporarily that poets are remarkable for being able to convey three or four or seven ideas in a single phrase. Arnold's nineteenth-century pronouncements perhaps bear some responsibility. Poetry contains "the breath and finer spirit of all knowledge"; it is "nothing less than the most perfect speech of man, that in which he comes nearest to being able to utter the truth," and "Poetry is the reality, philosophy the illusion," so that "most of what now passes with us for religion and philosophy will be replaced by poetry": such claims may well have prepared the apotheosis. A critic who has been impressed by welcome assurances that his subject has unsurpassed value might well aspire to become a member of an "in" group which occupies the heady summit of wisdom. Although the physicists and sociologists receive the largest governmental subsidies and the politicians and capitalists wield the great power, it is really he who is superior.

Since my purpose here is to discuss criticism, I shall not undertake to examine the claims of literature to wisdom. I grant readily that literature, including poetry, does possess wisdom of an important kind, and I have tried twice to define what the kind is.[2] I do not intend to go over that ground again and want only to suggest that we will be better critics if we resist the temptation to exalt ourselves above other men of intelligence and good will. *Maximos quosque scholasticos maxime stultos esse solere.* We ought, I say again, to respect the general reading public sufficiently to explain both our meanings and our reasons for thinking them tenable. If the consequence is some loss of enigmatic richness, the exposure of the substructure of our thought will assist critical progress by permitting assault on our evidence, or logic, or assumptions.

In what I have just said I have been thinking mainly of criticism published in certain books and in magazines other than "scholarly." But the assumption that literature is almost illimitably profound must also be responsible for the otherwise unaccountable assumption, in the most impeccably academic journals, that whatever meanings we can detect in a piece of creative writing must inevitably have been intended by the author—and this despite widespread lip-service to a principle expressed in Wimsatt and Beardsley's "The Intentional Fallacy." The author, who because he is a creative artist has the kind of wisdom just described, cannot have been unaware of anything that happens inside his work.

The evidence is overwhelming. Some years ago a perceptive essay on Milton made the point that, since an evil action must proceed from a poisoned will, no transition from innocence to guilt can be found in *Paradise Lost.* The claim, if perhaps not quite true of the poem—Milton would have said that sin can result from a sudden relaxation of the will as well as from a gradual poisoning of it—on its own terms has a certain cogency. The author, however, drops in such phrases as "Milton was preoccupied, I think, in . . . ," "What he wanted us to understand was . . . ," "Milton has conceived all along of . . . ," and the like, all implying that Milton carefully and deliberately built in a meaning—that Adam and Eve were already fallen at their creation—which until 1953 no reader had been able to perceive. A brilliant recent book on Milton argues that Milton makes his readers sin again and again as they progress through the epic, causing them to react favorably to a speech of Satan's which is then sharply denounced, to misinterpret the implications of similes, and generally

---

[2] See especially *Literature and the Irrational* (Englewood Cliffs, N. J., 1965, and New York, 1966), Chapter 8; but also "Matthew Arnold's Humanism: Literature as a Criticism of Life," *Studies in English Literature,* II (Autumn 1962), 385–402.

to misread and feel guilt, so that by the time they come to the end they are convicted of their own fallibility and accept involvement in the Parents' sin. All very well—I think the readings are mostly valid. The author, however, again insists, this time on the basis of evidence which comes not from literary theory or criticism but from theology, that the accomplishment was cleverly contrived and wholly conscious. We cannot take it for granted that principles accepted in one intellectual area are at once seen to have implications for another. Naive theories of the transfer of learning were refuted decades ago by psychologists.

I speak feelingly on the subject because it has repeatedly been assumed that my own critical interpretations must have been intended as readings of the authors' conscious purposes. One example will have to suffice. My recently published book on Milton, called *Unpremeditated Verse: Feeling and Perception in Paradise Lost*, was of course read by a press expert whose report said in the first paragraph, "The book is essentially a study of Milton's style in *Paradise Lost*, from the point of view of its (supposedly intended) effect." When I had read so far I was inundated by an enormous fatigue. And I wrote back, pointing out the implications of the title and citing six passages which either said or plainly implied that all the readings were *not* supposedly intended. What I found I thought was authentically present; but why should I have submitted myself to the risk of asserting that Milton was thinking while he wrote about exactly the things I saw when I looked?

The principle I am trying to argue is absurdly simple and obvious. I recently had lunch with a colleague in his office. Hanging on the wall was a "design" made by one of his sons—something like a fragment of a church window, with differently colored segments of curving shapes fitted into a long panel. "Did you ever see a woman in that?" I asked him; and I pointed her out. But nothing was further from my thought than asserting that the son, who to be sure is presumably subject to what a retired colleague once called "the mysterious working of the gonads," meant to hide a naked woman in his panel.

The point need not be labored. When a writer is fully caught up in his work, he senses fitnesses for which, unless his mind is exceptionally analytic, he feels it unnecessary to construct elaborate justifications: this has to go there because he *knows* it to be necessary. The critic, whose specialty I think should be understanding and explaining, can sometimes perceive the necessity and in the course of doing so discover a valid but unintended meaning. Although at times his subject may be precisely the author's conscious purposes, it need not always be that; and when it is not he will be wise to point to the artifact without psychoanalyzing the artist.

The same misconception about total awareness takes a different form in a very large number of critical articles and books which investigate historical backgrounds. What a scholar learns by laborious investigation to have preexisted a literary work, or better still, to have coexisted with it he almost regularly believes to have been known to his author and consciously used by him. Again illustrations abound, although again I shall suppress names. (None of the examples which follow are made up.)

A scholar, let us say, has been working on the ars moriendi tradition, to which his attention has been called by somebody else's study. He has made a considerable investment of time and effort in his research and naturally wants to find it useful, with the result that he attempts to place Marvell's "To His Coy Mistress" in the ars moriendi context, pointing as evidence to the fact that Marvell dwells briefly on death. The carpe diem tradition of course urges enjoyment of the present precisely because death is known to impend. Or, again, a skillful student of George Eliot is struck by the name "Adam" in Adam Bede and makes an intuitive guess that Eliot had Paradise Lost in the back of her mind as a model. "Like Milton's Michael," he proceeds to argue, "Dinah . . . appears only after the course of events can no longer be halted." This might be said of any fictive character who arrives too late to do something. "In Adam Bede, even more than in Paradise Lost, it is hindsight, and not foresight, which must yield the higher meaning." But this is of course true of most literary works which have any depth. And so on.

This kind of approach is just now very common; although I have no statistical evidence, a comparatively large number of dissertations recently completed or in progress appear to use some variation of it. Conrad's Heart of Darkness, it has been argued, is built up episode by episode, locale by locale, on the basis of Dante's Divine Comedy. My own current research, a book on Hermes Trismegistus, was provoked by a wholly unconvincing seminar paper on Marvell's "Upon Appleton House" as a Hermetic poem. The same vein is worked by established and often admirable scholars. Louis Martz's writings on the influence of meditative techniques derived from Ignatius Loyola's Spiritual Exercises exemplify this kind of thing at its best; but there is always a temptation to work the technique for a little more than its value. Probably young scholars all over the country are now busily proving that Renaissance poems traditionally classified as something else are really meditative. Some such discoveries are undoubtedly real, and helpful; others are dubious. A year ago, at a lecture on witchcraft by Rossell Hope Robbins, I discovered with surprise that the audience included persons who either thought they were witches or believed they knew witches. In a hundred or two hundred years, will some eager researcher propose that in the mid-twentieth century witchcraft was common and is the real, though disguised, subject of poems by Richard Wilbur and Marianne Moore?

The tendency for scholarly knowledge to spread into irrelevant areas is no doubt inevitable. Once the rose has been interpreted as a medieval symbol of a desirable woman, all the roses in literature risk being metamorphosed into women. The rose tree in Yeats's poem of that name stands for Ireland; but one would not be astonished to find it interpreted as a woman in an examination paper written by a student who had recently heard a lecture on *The Romance of the Rose* in a Chaucer course. Keys to literary works are apparently attractive because they are substitutes for close attention to the total content and they simultaneously offer reassurance by permitting reliance on other people's authority.

One final misuse of historical information appears in an uncritical subservience to data bearing on a work's genesis. Emily Dickinson's "A Route of Evanescence" will illustrate:

> A route of evanescence
> With a revolving wheel;
> A resonance of emerald,
> A rush of cochineal;
> And every blossom on the bush
> Adjusts its tumbled head. . . .

The poem concludes: "The mail from Tunis, probably, / An easy morning's ride." There is manuscript evidence that the subject of this poem is a hummingbird, and all academic comments on it known to me assume that interpretation. It may have been, and indeed probably was, the one intended by the author. My own first interpretation of the poem, however, after a few minutes of puzzlement, was "Of course —sunrise!" This reading is at least as faithful to the poem's content as the other. The most awkward detail is the revolving wheel. Although the sun appears wheel-shaped and revolves about the earth, "hummingbird" fits better here. On the other side, "The mail from Tunis, probably," is bad poetry if written about a hummingbird, which because it darts and hangs instead of making long straight runs does not give the impression of having come from a great distance or of being bound anywhere. But it is accurate to say that the sun which has risen at Tunis at, say, four o'clock in the morning arrives in New England well before noon. One may therefore argue quite plausibly that no matter what Miss Dickinson thought about as she wrote, she ought to have been thinking of sunrise.

The point to be made about the example is double. First, what a poem "means" is not necessarily what it was meant to mean. Meaning has reference not only to a speaker but also to a hearer. Reading, or even studying, this poem need not, as a matter of routine, involve doing "research." Nothing could more effectively kill literature—and especially, perhaps, poetry, which often stimulates interest and joy directly from the printed page—than the dissemination, by critics and teachers, of a notion that several hours of hard work must precede any perception of meaning. It does not, of course, follow that the association with the hummingbird should be excluded from a class discussion. No doubt it should come in; but not in such a way as to depress or discomfit a student who had decided that the subject is sunrise. Secondly, academic critics are astonishingly resistant to demands that they not use knowledge they have painfully acquired. In trying to win converts to my interpretation of the poem, I have found that the usual response is not "But she *meant* a hummingbird"; it is rather "It *can't mean* sunrise." When we think we know something (I fear), our minds tend to close, and thereafter we are unable to look at the object fairly. Whatever may be said of the scholar, the critic (I think), however well informed—and the more informed the better—ought to be able to deal comfortably with perceptions not mediated by learning.

An easy extension of this principle, that outside sources of information ought to be resorted to only when first-hand contact with the text creates puzzlement, will not work. When Shakespeare has Othello say about his courtship of Desdemona, "Upon this hint I spake," no difficulty is apparent, and the teacher (or editor, by means of a footnote) must explain that "hint" then often meant "occasion" or "opportunity." The matter has some importance because Othello must not be thought to have thrown the onus for beginning the courtship upon his wife. Edgar Wind's interpretation of Botticelli's *Primavera*, in *The Pagan Mysteries in the Renaissance*, is a comparable, if much more intricate, instance from a sister art. Nevertheless the principle that an expression or a whole literary work may "really" mean something the author did not suspect is unaffected.

A second, and final, example will also suggest the ease with which perceptiveness—of immense importance to criticism—can be neutralized by habit. Everybody knows Herrick's "When as in silks my *Julia* goes," but not everybody will have read the second stanza with the emphases I indicate by capitals:

> NEXT, when I cast mine eyes and see
> That brave Vibration each way FREE:
> O how THAT glittering taketh me!

In the first stanza Julia is clothed; in the second she is naked. I cannot tell how common the reading is, although surely a minority of teachers, at least, note the sharp contrasts. The point is again that when on several occasions I have discussed the interpretation with colleagues, it has been next to impossible to elicit an admission that the reading is acceptable. Once more I think my reading "correct," and this time by authorial intention; but minds have been made up in advance. Nobody has retorted "But the title is 'Upon Julia's Clothes.'" Whether the title was Herrick's is anybody's guess; but the demurrer would at least have critical relevance.

The relation between criticism and scholarship must detain us for another moment. Ideally, as I have implied, the critic should know everything connected with the subject he intends to discuss. Since criticism is a fiercely competitive activity, ignorance can become terribly embarrassing; but the important thing is that it may lead to serious distortions. An acquaintance with backgrounds is of course more necessary in proportion as the writing is temporally or cognitively remote. Yet for specific purposes accurate perception of what goes on within the work is an acceptable substitute for historical scholarship. Leslie Fiedler writes as follows in the preface to *Love and Death in the American Novel:*

The lack of footnotes and formal bibliography will advise the wary that I have sought everywhere the kind of validity which depends not on faithfulness to "fact" but on insight and sensitivity to nuance. I do not mean, of course, that I have despised accuracy (within the limits of my approach and temperament I have sought it) but that I have tried to produce a literary rather than a scientific work, a labor of love rather than one of patience.

The claim is not quite ingenuous. Fiedler knows a great deal about not only the books he discusses but also their authors and American literature generally. Nonetheless, it is quite true that faithful observation of literary details demands as much discipline as historical scholarship and deserves as much respect. Since it requires a native aptitude as well as hard work, it is perhaps rarer than good scholarship. In scholarly criticism the danger is that the work may be seen through a fog of irrelevant knowledge; in criticism like Fiedler's the risk is that perception will be skewed by energies originating in the critic's psyche. In theory, the ideal reader is one whose senses are preternaturally acute and whose memory is stored with all the necessary information about backgrounds but who is willing and able, at initial contact with the work, to present to it a *tabula rasa* upon which it may impress its meanings and patterns.

Like most ideals, this one is unattainable. Moreover, for a special purpose the critic may close his awareness to all data not of a preselected kind; and from point to point he will have to retire from direct contact in order to sort his perceptions, give them an order different from that in which he has received them, and by subordinating some to others achieve an expository structure. No purpose would be served by *merely* perceiving. The best stimulus to the "right" perceptions would be the work itself. But as an astigmatic sees everything asquint, the insightful critic who is hipped on sex, or metaphors, or ambiguities, or the superiority of intuition to reason, or, indeed, has any psychic peculiarity (and who has not?) may make unfaithful transcripts which have value, at least at certain points, rather as confession than as criticism.

In beginning to point toward a conclusion, I propose first that criticism should always give evidence or reasons for its assertions. If it does not do so, it may sound impressive but in fact is not likely much to advance human understanding. What is most unacceptable is *obiter dicta* which claim truth because of the exceptional keenness of the critic's mind. Let him, I urge, put the foundations of his judgments in plain sight so that we can decide for ourselves whether he is reliable. For centuries physical scientists were contented with unexamined *aperçus* and inferences from principles accepted on authority. At present criticism only occasionally contributes to real knowledge because its insights are not painfully validated and its orthodoxies are accepted on faith.

What constitutes evidence, we must observe next, differs widely from essay to essay or from book to book; and it is here that "scholarship" most frequently errs. The filling of a critique with masses of unquestionable fact may have nothing to do with the establishment of its thesis. As I have pointed out elsewhere, John Matthews Manly was probably wrong in assuming that because Chaucer's *Manciple's*

Tale is rhetorically more highly elaborated than, say, *The Miller's Tale* it must have been written earlier. Manly took it for granted that all true literary progress is in the direction of greater realism—a proposition now unlikely to win assent. Students often incautiously perpetrate similar errors. A number of years ago I was given a senior paper on *Samson Agonistes* which argued that because Samson was in low estate when we first meet him the play could not be a tragedy. The long demonstration that he was indeed in prison, blinded, scorned, and taunted failed to bear on the major thesis, that in "true" tragedy the curve of the protagonist's fate is downward. The fault is surprisingly common. According to an old story, an Indian fakir who had been locked into a room made his exit through the keyhole, leaving only his loincloth behind. "And if you don't believe it," concluded the teller, "here is the loincloth." Much painstaking academic criticism proves its major conclusions in ways no more convincing than this.

In criticism not intended as "scholarly"—for example, Fiedler's book—demonstration requires the showing of data in the literary work adequate to validate the asserted qualities. This can be, and sometimes is, achieved brilliantly. What is necessary is the bringing into sharp focus of stimuli which affect us without usually attracting our attention, as we may feel a room to be cool without noticing that its dominant color is blue. What I am thinking of is a capability in the critic analogous to that of a visually acute man not only to see, but to make visible to others, the violets and greens and reds of the shadows in a portrait, where the unskilled observer sees only grays. All *aperçus* which tell us something about the literary object (and not merely about the percipient) ought, in theory, to be justifiable in this way. Sometimes the critic may intuit justly although he is unable to explain why. If so, his statement is sound although unsupported, and the reader who can himself provide evidence for it may elect charitably to do so. But he need not, and I think it is arrogant for the critic to expect him to. Ordinarily, the failure to support critical pronouncements implies inability even when the critic thinks that the giving of reasons would be otiose; but it may sometimes derive from self-importance. Since I conceive highly of criticism, I want it to perform a valuable human function and not to be vitiated by superciliousness or portentousness.

As has been indicated, reasoning is often as essential as evidence. The kind of evidence to be offered must often be shown to be the right kind to achieve a specific end; or the central argument may assume the correctness of a prior belief which must be made plausible;

and the relationships between differing stages of the analysis must be explained. Unfortunately, keen perceptivity is not always accompanied by logical rigor. The critical situation would be much less confused than it is if every critic knew accurately from what part of the entire panoply of critical possibility each of his own discussions was drawn. As things are, the really fundamental critical issues of our period are obscured by seldom being faced. Most valuable of all would be substantial agreement about what literature is and therefore about what aspects of it most deserve critical exploration. To be helpful, however, the orthodox aesthetic would have to be verified both empirically and dialectically by a group effort extending over many years. The present orthodoxies in both scholarship and criticism seem to me to have been adopted far too easily.

I end by offering a tentative manifesto:

1. The truth, falsity, or partial truth of every intuition can be established, ultimately, by the gathering and correct interpretation of relevant evidence, provided only that the intuition is objective in being focused on the qualities of an aesthetic object. (Although possibly unsound, this principle must be affirmed in order to be tested.)

2. Intuitions not so validated must be regarded as dubious—at best, only provisionally or hypothetically true. (But of course hypotheses can sometimes be advanced as hypotheses in criticism as in physical science.)

3. No tonal claim to authority, as, for example, by stylistic impressiveness, a show of breezy self-confidence, or an ironic manner which implies superiority, has cognitive weight, since it reveals only that the critic's estimate of his own abilities is high or his gamesmanship skillful.

4. To contribute to validation, evidence must bear upon the gist of the assertion with which it is connected and not upon the assertion's periphery or upon some corollary drawn from it.

5. It cannot regularly be assumed that knowledge possessed by an author's contemporaries must have been known to him or that, having it, he must have used it in the work under consideration.

In brief, criticism has arrived (I think) at the point which physical science had reached about the time Bishop Sprat issued his famous call for a simple and factual prose. Enormous progress has been made and prospects for the future are bright; but critics still exist who, like the Hermetist John Everard in 1650, claim implicitly to have been made wise by revelation. I do not propose to silence them; men have a right to their heresies, and what is negligible as criticism may have some other value. I suggest, however, that criticism recognize its primary allegiance to itself and to literature and urge that the authority of critics depends not on oracular utterance but on the demonstrated soundness of their views.

These five points are a beginning; but they may be badly misinterpreted unless an additional set of cautionary precepts is added.

1. Creative writing has its own body of potential subject matter and its own kinds of truth. Unlike science, it has no necessary responsibility to factual truth, although it may sometimes elect to assert that it mirrors actuality, or some portion of actuality, faithfully.

2. A scientific criticism, to be relevant to literature, cannot assume that whatever can be proved has literary significance but must seek truths appropriate to the real nature of its subject matter. (I do not anticipate being much enlightened by a cascade of data issuing from computers unless aesthetic qualities and values can somehow be quantified.)

3. Progress therefore depends upon a more adequate aesthetic than has so far been attained; but because art may propose for itself a wide variety of legitimate aims, the aesthetic must be formulated in very abstract terms. Arguments for a special kind of art—for example, literary realism or a colloquial diction in poetry—must be recognized as programmatic and not descriptive.

4. The ultimate, although perhaps unattainable, goal is an aesthetic which will be corroborated by a total philosophy that finds a unique role for art in the entire range of potential human activities. At most, I suspect that we can hope only for temporarily adequate formulations. But in science too all general laws are subject to revaluation.

It is a formidable program, and no doubt in need of much revision; but it will serve as a start. Whatever the ultimate program might be, no one critic will be able to do much toward fulfilling it. We may hope, however, that a cooperative effort, carried on no doubt mainly in the colleges and universities, where responsibility can be demanded, by men who do not quickly conceive that they have discovered final answers, may permit a gradual advance.

University of California, Berkeley

GEORG LUKÁCS: THE PROBLEMS OF DIALECTICAL CRITICISM

Stephen G. Nichols, Jr.

In the entire history of literary criticism, it is doubtful whether any professional critic has tried to circumscribe literature within such radically narrow limits as those set down by the Hungarian critic Georg Lukács.[1] The literary achievements of the past, the aspirations of the present and future have been, are, and will be the result of a single mode, realism,[2] and, to all intents and purposes, a single genre, the novel. Moreover, so far as the achievements of the past are concerned, there are only a very few authors who can be truly said to have realized the critical ideals espoused by Lukács. Among the authors of the last century and a half, these giants include only Scott, Balzac, Tolstoy, Mann, and to a lesser degree Goethe, Keller, Stendhal, Dostoevsky, and Gorky.

The historical, personal, and intellectual reasons underlying Lukács' espousal of so circumscribed a critical system have been traced by Peter Demetz in his excellent book, *Marx, Engels, and the Poets*,[3]

---

[1] A shorter version of this paper was read to the General Topics 6 Section (Literature and Society) of the MLA on December 28, 1967. I wish to acknowledge the advice and encouragement of Professor Germaine Brée, who invited me to participate in the General Topics conference on Lukács and Aragon.

[2] "We are thus concerned with a definition of realism according to which Homer and Sophocles, Dante and Rabelais, Cervantes and Shakespeare, Goethe and E. T. A. Hoffmann, Pushkin and Balzac, Tolstoy and Gorky—while representing various historical trends and stages of realism—are all representative of the great school of realism." Lukács, "On Socialist Realism," *International Literature* [*Soviet Literature*], No. 4 (1939), p. 87.

[3] Chicago, 1967. Although the English edition is a translation, by Jeffrey L. Sammons, of the original *Marx, Engels und die Dichter* (Stuttgart, 1959), it

and need not concern us here. What might be profitably attempted, however, is a description of the critical act *chez* Lukács; an analysis which will offer some insight into the nature of the perception of literature that the reader might be expected to gain from reading what one English observer has termed "this thundering good critic of the classical novel."[4]

One of the first factors to emerge from the experience of reading Lukács is the awareness one has of participating in a powerful dialectic whose objective is the situation of the literary object in a larger historical and sociological context. This is natural, for Lukács will maintain that the superiority of the Marxist viewpoint consists precisely in its capacity to take a comprehensive view of man: nothing exists in isolation, and it would be misleading to study the literary object only in relation to other literary works. Lukács respects the influence of literary tradition as much as anyone else and will acknowledge its influential role in the creative process. Nevertheless, literature stands in a conspicuous relationship to the historical moment in which it was created, and to the "march of reality"[5] to which the creative moment belongs. Since literature bears witness to the totality of society and its patterns of development, criticism can do no less than to reveal the full perspective, the potentiality of the literary object it studies.

The first element in most of Lukács' literary essays, then, constitutes nothing more nor less than a discussion of the presupposition which will inform and shape the whole critical effort. This stage may be implicit or explicit, but it surely will be present, taking the form of an affirmation of the Marxist philosophy of history as the only system competent to analyze man as a whole, the only true vision of the completeness of human endeavor throughout the ages. Lukács may state the presupposition specifically in terms of Marxist ideology:

Things now face us in a clear, sharp light which to many may seem cold and hard; a light shed on them by the teachings of Marx. Marxism searches for the material roots of each phenomenon, regards them in their historical connections and movement, ascertains the laws of such movement and

---

contains some material not found in the original. Thus Mr. Demetz has taken advantage of the translation to discuss the first two volumes of Lukács' *Aesthetik* (Berlin, 1963).

[4] "The Mirror of Reality," *Times Literary Supplement*, Sept. 22, 1950, p. 591.

[5] *Essays on Thomas Mann* (New York, 1965), p. 15.

demonstrates their development from root to flower, and in so doing lifts every phenomenon out of merely emotional, irrational, mystic fog and brings it to the bright light of understanding. . . .[6]

Or he may couch the presupposition in terms of the social reality of our time:

Ist doch—man könnte sagen: seit der Junischlacht 1848 des Pariser Proletariats—der Kampf von Sozialismus and Kapitalismus das grundlegende Problem der Epoche, in der wir leben. Es ist deshalb selbstverständlich, dass auch Literatur und Literaturtheorie diese Tatsache widerspiegeln müssen.[7]

To the careful reader, the polemical overtones of such statements are inescapable: the affirmation of the Marxist view of history requires a concomitant condemnation of opposing views. Almost invariably, the first phase of the dialectic will postulate an opposition between the Marxist historical perspective and a negative counterpart of this view, consisting of various modernist literary systems depicted as actively hostile to the Marxist viewpoint and methodology:

"But all this is long out of date," the modernists cry. "All this is the undesirable, outworn legacy of the nineteenth century," say those who—intentionally or unintentionally, consciously or unconsciously—support the Fascist ideology and its pseudo-revolutionary rejection of the past, which is in reality a rejection of culture and humanism. Let us look without prejudice at the bankruptcy of the very latest philosophies; let us consider how most philosophers of our day are compelled to pick up the broken and scattered fragments of dialectic (falsified and distorted in this decomposition) whenever they want to say something even remotely touching its essence about present-day life; let us look at the modern attempts at a philosophical synthesis and we shall find them miserable, pitiful caricatures of the old genuine dialectic, now consigned to oblivion.[8]

---

[6] *Studies in European Realism* (New York, 1964), p. 1.

[7] *Wider den missverstandenen Realismus* (Hamburg, 1958), p. 8. (The English translation, *Realism in Our Time* [New York, 1964], does not include the introduction from which the above quotation was taken.) For similar formulations, see the introduction to *Die Grablegung des alten Deutschland* (Munich, 1967), and "In Search of Modern Man" and "The Tragedy of Modern Art," in *Essays on Thomas Mann*.

[8] *Studies in European Realism*, p. 4. See also such remarks as: "The artistic 'vanguard' of the era of imperialism has indeed come forward again and again with slogans that have been represented as 'revolutionary slogans,' calling for a

It would be a mistake to assume that the opposition between socialist and bourgeois world views developed at this stage of the dialectic is somehow inessential to the literary study which will follow. Lukács believes that "content determines form," and that there is "no content of which man himself is not the focal point."[9] The statement of presupposition thus functions to remind the reader that literary study, like any cognitive pursuit, can only be meaningful in terms of the total picture of man in the modern world. In other words, the proper study of literature postulates a definite perspective, a perspective enabling the reader, with the help of the critic, to see "society and history for what they are," and the literary object for what it reveals of this truth.[10]

Having established the requisite perspective in this way, Lukács will turn to consider the specific literary problem or work proposed for a given study. The chief characteristic of the dialectic in this second phase is its *progressively expanding focus*. Whatever the point of departure for the discussion of a literary work, we shall have progressed before long from the original point of emphasis, the discussion of narrative techniques in Balzac or Zola, for example, to quite another sphere of interest, e.g., a discussion of the survival of feudal practices in post-revolutionary France. The important point to consider here is the effortlessness of the transition from the literary object to the historical one. We have to do truly with an expansion of the same field of vision, the same focus, and not with a shift from one sphere of knowledge to another. Clearly, such could not be the case if the dialectic did not play a significant role in transforming the various components of the perception.

Lukács relies on two main resources to make the expanding field of vision successful. In the first place, the presupposition or affirmation of the world view in the initial phase of the dialectic has prepared us for just such an enlarging of the field of inquiry as we experience when historico-sociological concerns are superposed upon the literary discussion. Secondly, the dialectic itself presents the various objects of study in such a way as to enhance the comparison the critic seeks to make. Subtly but inexorably, the dialectic reshapes the objects so as

---

revolutionary annihilation of the inherited art which has supposedly lost its value in modern life and has allegedly become a brake on the development of the new man" ("On Socialist Realism," p. 88).

[9] *Realism in Our Time*, p. 19.

[10] "Perspective" is a key concept for Lukács, who uses it in a number of different ways. In this initial sense, however, it functions in its broadest connotation. See *Realism in Our Time*, p. 97.

to facilitate their intended *rapprochement:* Lukács' description of the literary object will be such as to suggest quite naturally its similarity to or dependence upon the historical description that constitutes the expansion of focus. The process is not metaphoric, but metonymic; from the perspective of the expanded focus one realizes that the earlier discussion of the literary object was simply the substance, the core of the containing socio-historical viewpoint that has been dialectically established.

The reshaping of the literary object begins quite simply by a deft turning of our attention away from the work as a "read work," i.e., away from the contemplation of the experience of perception and its correlates. Instead, we come to accept the work as a described object. This constitutes an important step because it removes us, for the purposes of the dialectic, from the necessity of independent experience of the work; or, rather, direct experience of the work may be irrelevant to the perspective created by the description. The function of the description, in fact, consists precisely in transforming the work of art from something which can be independently perceived as artifact, having an essential meaning of its own, to something which can and must be perceived in terms of an expanded context.

Lest there be doubt that the dialectic does not transform the work of art in a radical manner, let us examine briefly the relationship Lukács postulates between the various components of the literary object, the author, and the real world. The technique of transformation, although undeniably rooted in the perspective established by the presupposition, relies for its success upon the rhetorical skill of the critic. Of the many forms used for this purpose, one of the most successful is the juxtaposition of a portion of the literary work under discussion with an historical or economic anecdote. The following example, from Lukács' discussion of Balzac's *Les Paysans,* offers a good example of the dynamics of transformation:

Montcornet [one of the principal characters in the book] wants to do away with all the traditional rights of the poor: the right to gather brushwood in the forest, the right to glean in the fields after harvest. The abolition of these rights is a necessary concomitant of the capitalist transformation of the large estates. A few years before Balzac's novel was published, Karl Marx, then a young man, put up a bitter fight in the columns of the *Rheinische Zeitung* against the Wood Theft Bill which was before the Rhenish Diet and which proposed to abolish similar ancient rights.[11]

---

[11] *Studies in European Realism,* p. 35.

The expansion of focus is subtle but inexorable. It assures that the literary object itself will be subsumed into the larger historical problems of the period. Thus when we refocus on the literary object, it will be not in terms suggested by the work itself, the contemplation of which we have never really undertaken, but rather in terms of the perspective created by the description.

Immediately following the above quotation, for example, Lukács returns to the discussion of *Les Paysans* in the following manner:

In this question, Balzac definitely takes sides with Montcornet. In order to defend Montcornet's attitude, he picks on cases in which the brushwood-gatherers cut down or deliberately injured growing trees. But it is clear that Montcornet's action is directed not against abuses of these rights, but against the ancient rights themselves. Montcornet gives orders that only those peasants be permitted to glean who are provided with a certificate of indigence by the authorities; he also sees to it that the results of the gleaning should be as meager as possible. This shows that Montcornet, well trained in Pomerania [where he has been an officer with Napoleon's army of occupation], is quite determined to do away with these remnants of feudalism. The peasants on the Montcornet estate are in a position in which "all the brutality of primitive forms of society is combined with all the torments and miseries of civilized countries" (Marx). . . . Balzac here gives us a masterly picture of the tragedy of the peasant smallholding. He presents in literary form the same essential development of the post-revolutionary smallholding that Marx described in the *Eighteenth Brumaire*.[12]

It is evident that, so far as dialectical purposes are concerned, Balzac, Montcornet, Marx, and Lukács himself have ceased to be persons and characters of varying degrees of historical and literary reality. They have been joined in the same descriptive dimension to become participants in a dialectical affirmation of the laws of historical progress as demonstrated in the condition of the peasant smallholding.

The basis for the dialectical transformation of author, literary characters, and historical figures constitutes one of the fundamental principles of Lukács' critical theory and practice. It is the notion of *Weltanschauung*, a concept underlying almost all of Lukács' prescriptive, evaluative, and theoretical statements about literature. Despite the central importance of the concept, its implications, in terms of the

---

[12] *Ibid.*

relationship postulated between the critic's perception of the work and his judgment of it, have not been fully explored.

Lukács uses the notion of *Weltanschauung* in several special ways, but primarily to render concrete the theoretical statements of the presupposition that a literary work must have a special relationship to objective reality, a relationship that need not be one intended by the author. Indeed, it is a maxim of Lukács' notion of critical realism that the world view of a novel of critical realism will be quite different from the author's personal views. Dissociation of the author as spokesman for his work, a principle which underlies most criticism in one form or another, turns out to be only the beginning in Lukács' dialectic. Many times he will make use of the technique of polar opposition that we have already witnessed to postulate an active opposition between the world view represented by the author, and the "correct" reflection of objective reality found in his work:

Undoubtedly, there is a certain contradiction here between Scott's directly political views and his artistic world picture. He, too, like so many great realists, such as Balzac or Tolstoy, became a great realist despite his own political and social views. In Scott, too, one can establish Engels's "triumph of realism" over his personal, political and social views. Sir Walter Scott, the Scottish petty aristocrat, automatically affirms this development with a sober rationality. Scott, the writer, on the other hand, embodies the sentiment of the Roman poet, Lucan: "Victrix causa diis placuit, sed victa Catoni" (the victorious cause pleased the gods, but the vanquished pleased Cato).[13]

In other words, the critic will not be able to speak of the author's intention, his meaning, because intention remains under the control of an erroneous world view. The quality of greatness for historical writers like Scott, or critical realists like Balzac and Thomas Mann, lies precisely in the "discrepancy between intention and performance."[14]

Lukács does not make the dissociation between intention and performance gratuitously. By showing that the author actually stands between the work and its correct interpretation, Lukács can argue persuasively that the focus of critical attention can and must be on the

---

[13] *The Historical Novel* (Boston, 1963), p. 54. See also *Studies in European Realism*, Chapters One and Three; the principle underlies the discussions of Thomas Mann, as well, to name but one other well-known study.

[14] *Studies in European Realism*, p. 21.

relationship between the characters and the reality they reflect. Lukács thus minimizes the author's ontological status in the work in favor of an emphatic valuation of the literary characters. Once accepted as representative of reality, that is, reality independent of their creator's mind, the characters may be seen as the principal conveyer of meaning in the novel. They are valued as the antithesis of the author's subjective, and thus unreal, intentionality.

To achieve the requisite valuation of literary characters, Lukács naturally relies upon the concept of Weltanschauung. Thanks to their world view, fictional beings may attain an ontological status in terms of the reality they represent just like any other historical personage. The critic may, in fact, talk about Julien Sorel's or Rastignac's relationship to post-revolutionary France just as easily as he can discuss Victor Hugo's or Henri Beyle's relationship to the same period. The basis for this technique was laid down in one of Lukács' key articles written during the formative period of the 'thirties, when many of his philosophical and political theories were first applied to literature. The article in question, "The Intellectual Physiognomy of Literary Characters,"[15] first remarks upon the tremendous vitality Plato succeeded in imparting to the Symposium thanks to the lively dialogue he places in the mouths of the famous, historical figures who participate in the work. It is clear from Lukács' remarks that he feels Plato to have succeeded in making the historical figures come alive in their own right: "Socrates, Alcibiades, Aristophanes and many others stand before us as living individuals . . . . this dialogue gives us not only ideas, but living characters whose feelings we can share . . . ."[16]

As he continues, one realizes the full extent of the existential autonomy Lukács seeks to grant to literary characters. They are treated almost as though they were historical figures, capable of independent thought and action.[17] Thus Lukács speaks of the characters' "whole personality" as being

concentrated in the thinking process, in the clarifying of this problem and

---

[15] The English translation, by Leonard E. Mins, was published in *International Literature* [Soviet Literature], No. 8 (1936), pp. 55–83.

[16] *Ibid.*, p. 55.

[17] "Scott's great art consists precisely in *individualizing his historical heroes* in such a way that certain, *purely individual traits of character*, quite peculiar to *them*, are brought into a very complex, *very live* relationship with the age *in which they live*, with the movement which they represent and endeavor to lead to victory" (italics mine; *The Historical Novel*, p. 47). Similarly, he describes Stendhal's Mathilde de la Mole as though she were an historical personage of

thinking it out to the end. This quintessence arising before us, this way of thinking, enables Plato to make the way in which each of his characters approaches the problem, what he assumes as an axiom not requiring proof, what he proves and how he proves it, the abstract heights that his thinking reaches, the source of his concrete examples, what he ignores or omits, and how he does it, appear as the profound characteristic property of each and every one of them. A number of living persons stands before us, marked and unforgettable in their human individuality. . . .[18]

Lest there be any doubt that it is their *Weltanschauung* that confers on characters their status as quasi-independent existential beings, Lukács spells out the terms:

A description that does not include the *Weltanschauung* of the created characters cannot be complete. *Weltanschauung* is the highest form of consciousness; hence if the writer ignores it he blurs the most important thing in the figure he has in mind. *Weltanschauung is a profound personal experience of each and every person, an extremely characteristic expression of his inward nature,* and it likewise reflects in a very significant fashion the general problems of his age.[19]

Once accustomed to thinking of the characters as more or less complete personalities in themselves, the reader may accept an interpretation of them—and frequently of the novel in which they appear —in terms of the real historical events and movements they are said to represent. Lukács makes no difficulty about projecting the characters directly into the context of objective reality that their *Weltanschauungen* are said to guarantee. The author remains nominally present, of course, but only as a shadowy presence accepted as responsible for the world that, in fact, the critic unveils.[20]

the restoration: "Mathilde de la Mole is a sincere convinced monarchist who is passionately devoted to romantic monarchist ideals and who despises her own class because it lacks the devoted and passionate faith which burns in her own soul. She prefers the plebeian Julien Sorel, the passionate Jacobin and Napoleon-admirer, to the men of her own station" (*Studies in European Realism*, p. 79).

[18] "Intellectual Physiognomy," p. 55.

[19] *Ibid.*, p. 56.

[20] Besides the examples quoted already, we might note one further, taken from "The Tragedy of Modern Art," where Lukács discusses Thomas Mann's *Dr. Faustus*. Arguing that "the great world" portrayed in Goethe's *Faust* could no longer exist as a possibility in the Germany that emerged from the revolution of 1848, Lukács asserts that Mann's *Faustus*, since it "omits all the attempts of the working class to create a democratic 'great world' in Germany," is "a Faust

Implicit in the initial statement of presupposition discussed earlier was the assumption that the critic's perspective controls the interpretation of a novel not because of his perception of the inner world of the work, but because of his understanding of the outer world of objective reality. We saw that the dialectically expanded focus functioned to raise any discussion of the artistic work to the level of an historical and sociological containing world. From the same point of view, it is inevitable that the critic's determination of the historically containing world will naturally affect his selection of the *Weltanschauungen* to be discussed in any given novel. This is especially true since Lukács believes the *Weltanschauungen*, as we saw, to be precisely the place where the impact of reality will be felt in the inner, artistic world.

Hence those characters who can be shown to possess a *Weltanschauung* in conformity with the "objective reality" determined by the critic will obviously be singled out for discussion. Under the circumstances, their prominence in the critical discussion must inevitably derive more from the dialectical significance of their role in relation to the critic's perspective than from their role in terms of the work as a whole. In short, Lukács' methodology requires the establishment of an evaluative hierarchy of characters and ideas according to the support they lend to the critical perspective.

The principal aristocratic characters in *Ivanhoe*, for example, assume a secondary status beside the serfs in whose bearing Lukács discerns the real drama of the novel.[21] Similarly, when Lukács dis-

---

of the study." "It is in such a small world that Mann's Faustus tragedy takes place. And it can be a real tragedy, despite its deliberately tragi-comic features, because the study of the new Faust is made inaccessibly fast from the outside world; at least psychologically and morally. The intelligentsia with whom Mann's Faust, Adrian Leverkühn, comes into contact is rushing headlong into Fascist barbarism, performing a grotesque, snobbish death dance as it does so. He on the other hand lives a life of asceticism and otherworldly disdain. 'Unworldly' (*weltscheu*) most typically describes his response to the humanity of his day. But what is tragi-comic or, better, grotesquely tragic about his story is that, despite his self-imposed seclusion, the very themes he chooses for his work are most intimately related to the snobbish and reactionary tendencies of his time, if only in an ultimate sense. Next, his 'unworldliness,' his monk-like repudiation of the affairs of men in his day and age opens the very door to the devil in his work and life" (*Essays on Thomas Mann*, pp. 60–62).

[21] "Thus when Belinsky quite rightly says that Ivanhoe, the hero of this novel and likewise an aristocratic adherent of this compromise, is overshadowed by the minor characters, this formal problem of the historical novel has a very clear historical-political and popular content. For although one of the

cusses Stendhal's *Le Rouge et le noir*, Mathilde de la Mole appears to assume a greater importance than Mme. de Rênal, and, in the passage quoted (n. 17), becomes the optic through whom we are to understand the motivation of Julien Sorel himself. In the *Chartreuse de Parme*, Count Mosca, considered as a kind of upper class Vautrin, becomes the spokesman for the society against which Fabrice reacts by retiring to the charterhouse. Julien Sorel and Fabrice del Dongo must respectively be viewed through the historical perspective represented by other, less significant characters, while their own actions diminish into reaction against the stresses of the restoration world.[22]

But it is not only the selection of *Weltanschauungen* that must depend upon the critic's perspective. The valuation of *Weltanschauungen*, even the existence of a clearly defined world view ultimately fall under his jurisdiction. Gide, for example, cites the debate between Mithridates, Pharnace, and Xipharès, in Scene One, Act Three of Racine's *Mithridate*, as an impressive model of universal character portrayal in which the essential truth of each character stands out in bold relief against the magnitude of Mithridate's proposed challenge to Rome. Lukács contradicts Gide's assessment on the grounds that the attitudes expressed in Mithridate's great *tirade*, and in his sons' response to it, have not been shown to grow naturally out of the personal life of the characters. Sublimely indifferent to the dictates of the dramatic mode, Lukács argues that Racine does not trouble to portray the previous experiences of the characters in sufficient depth to explain how the "concrete arguments" propounded by the characters in this scene have been determined. As a result, "the intellectual dispute remains hanging in the air; it has no root in the

---

figures who overshadows Ivanhoe is his father, the brave and ascetic Saxon nobleman, Cedric, the most important of these figures are the latter's serfs, Gurth and Wamba, and above all the leader of the armed resistance to Norman rule, the legendary and popular hero, Robin Hood. The interaction between 'above' and 'below,' the sum of which constitutes the totality of popular life, is thus manifested in the fact that, while on the whole the historical tendencies 'above' receive a more distinct and generalized expression, we find the true heroism with which the historical antagonisms are fought out, with few exceptions, 'below' " (*The Historical Novel*, p. 49).

[22] "Stendhal created flesh and blood, the destinies of real men and women. What makes these men and women typical—although regarded superficially they are all extreme individual cases—is that these extreme cases incarnate the deepest longings of the best sons of the post-revolutionary *bourgeois* class" (*Studies in European Realism*, p. 81).

human passions of the characters and therefore cannot lend them any intellectual physiognomy."[23]

As though aware of the vulnerability of his methodology on this point, Lukács tries to argue that it will be the author's conception of the characters which will make "possible and necessary the intellectual level" capable of sustaining credible intellectual physiognomy.[24] This statement is based, however, on the following reasoning:

The portrayal of intellectual physiognomy always presupposes, therefore, an extraordinarily broad and profound, universal and human characterization of the figures. The level of thought far exceeds any commonplace potentiality, without however ever losing the character of personal expression. This presupposes, first of all, the continuous experiencing of the vital connection between the characters' personal experiences and their intellectual expression, i.e., the portrayal of thoughts as the process of life and not as its result.[25]

There are two levels of presupposition in this statement, i.e., references to objective criteria which supposedly can be singled out in any given text by any observant critic. Significantly, these "objective" elements of the text do not come naturally from consideration of the text itself, but are value judgments whose truth derives from their dialectical presentation by the critic. The critic and he alone in Lukács' system determines whether or not there is a "continuous experiencing of the vital connections between the characters' personal experiences and their intellectual expression."

Clearly, the result of the dialectic can only be to interpose the critic between the reader and the literary object. At every stage, those supposedly objective criteria, the historical context, the *Weltanschauungen* and so forth, turn out to depend, for their definition, upon the critic's own perspective. The circularity of interpretation leaves him in a world of subjective perception, a disconcerting enough situation for someone who considers himself a worshipper of reality independent of the mind of man. Nonetheless, the position is the inevitable consequence of his faith in the concrete objectivity of his-

---

[23] "Intellectual Physiognomy," p. 57.

[24] "The decline of literature is always expressed—possibly most strikingly in the modern age—in the blurring of intellectual physiognomy, the deliberate neglect or inability of the writer to post [sic] and solve this problem creatively." *Ibid.*, p. 56.

[25] *Ibid.*, p. 60.

tory. Unhappily for this viewpoint, history is even less self-evident than literature. The literary artifact may offer itself in its entirety to generation after generation; the historical event offers only physical and intellectual traces to succeeding generations.

Strictly speaking, it would distort Lukács' position to argue that, while he implies the self-evident quality of history, he actually speaks in these terms. Instead, he assumes the self-evidence of history *as perceived by* Hegel, Marx, Engels, and Lenin. Thus he does not quite praise Sir Walter Scott's novels because they conform to history, but because, after careful dialectical presentation, it transpires that "Scott's manner of composition shows a very interesting parallel to Hegel's philosophy of history."[26] Nevertheless, the fact that Lukács does not stand by himself in the middle of his interpretive circle does not alter the essentially solipsistic nature of his relationship to the work.

After what we have seen, it would appear impossible to deny that Lukács' methodology abandons all attempt to recapture any meaning other than what the critic's perspective brings to the work. Particularly, little or no grounds would seem to offer themselves for discussing the author's intention, in the sense of the symbolic meaning created in the writing of the work. How, for example, could we speak of a meaning inherent in the text itself, one present since the creation of the work, and one that can be verified intersubjectively by a number of readers, if the meaning of the work must inevitably be defined in terms of *Weltanschauungen* which are, in turn, determined by the critic? The latter would seem to indicate that the critic's intention, the critic's meaning rather than the author's, governed the interpretation of the work.

Lukács indicates that the path of transcendence from the critic's subjective judgment naturally lies in the intention of the work as seen in the form itself. Intention determines the form that will give it

---

[26] "For Hegel, too, the 'world-historical individual' arises upon the broad basis of the world of 'maintaining individuals.' 'Maintaining individuals' is Hegel's all-embracing term for men in 'civil society'; it describes society's uninterrupted self-reproduction through the activity of these individuals. The basis is formed by the personal, private, egoistic activity of individual human beings. In and through this activity the socially general asserts itself. In this activity the 'maintenance of moral life' unfolds itself" (*The Historical Novel*, p. 39). Inasmuch as Lukács interprets Scott's characters according to the Hegelian terminology, it is evident that the Hegelian view of history is more fundamental to Lukács' criticism than the experience of Scott's novels. This is surely one reason why reading Lukács on Scott is, alas, preferable to reading Scott himself.

expression; and by intention is meant "the intention realized in the work" which "need not coincide with the writer's conscious intention."[27] Nevertheless, intention must not be thought of as being manifested in formal categories:

It is the view of the world, the ideology or *Weltanschauung* underlying a writer's work, that counts. And it is the writer's attempt to reproduce this view of the world which constitutes his "intention" and is the formative principle underlying the style of a given piece of writing. Looked at in this way, style ceases to be a formalistic category. Rather it is rooted in content; it is the specific form of a specific content. Content determines form. But there is no content of which man himself is not the focal point. However various the *données* of literature . . . the basic question is, and will remain: what is Man?[28]

Admittedly, this statement looks more like a variation on the previous theme than a radical departure calculated to overcome the objection that the critic's intention, rather than the author's, constitutes the perspective of a Lukácsian dialectic. But before rejecting the claim of transcendent intentionality out of hand, let us look briefly at one of Lukács' studies in which the attempt is made to demonstrate precisely the thesis enunciated in the above quotation. Let us examine how Lukács, without falling into the formalist excesses of idealist stylistic critics like Vossler and Spitzer, would connect the style of a work of art and the *Weltanschauung* the author seeks to express through it.

In an article entitled, "Narration vs. Description: A Contribution to the Discussion on Naturalism and Formalism,"[29] Lukács undertakes a running critique of intentionality in Tolstoy and Zola based upon the observation of a difference in their manner of presentation. The point of departure is a commentary on the different form given by the respective authors to horse racing incidents which occur in Zola's *Nana* and Tolstoy's *Anna Karenina*. Zola's horse race, according to Lukács, stands in a purely fortuitous relationship to the plot of

---

[27] *Realism in Our Time*, p. 19.

[28] *Ibid.*

[29] *International Literature* [*Soviet Literature*], No. 6 (1937), pp. 96–112. "Idea and Form in Literature: Narration vs. Description," *Masses and Mainstream*, December 1949, pp. 40–61, is exactly the same article, and apparently the same translation.

Nana,[30] while Tolstoy's forms an essential part in the development of the novel's plot.[31]

On the basis of these contrasting observations, Lukács immediately formulates a series of questions designed to establish the necessary connection between "style" and intention. To provide this connection with a convincing conceptual valuation, Lukács introduces the terms "contingency" and "essentiality." He argues that the two horse-racing incidents, particularly when considered from the perspective of the plot as a whole, raise the question: What is essential and what contingent in artistic portrayal? On the one hand, contingency is a necessary element in any life-like portrayal, but on the other, the sequences within a work must stand in an essential relationship one to the other. Above all, essentiality consists not of completeness of self-contained description, but "of the relations of the characters towards the events in which they participate, by which their destinies are determined, and by means of which they perform their acts."[32]

Contingency thus functions as a negative value, associated with description, i.e., episodes, complete in themselves, giving a picture of important social phenomena. Essentiality, on the contrary, assumes a positive connotation, for it implies the narrative style by which an author demonstrates, through the tight interconnection of episode and thought, the dependence of the inner world of the novel on the external world of reality.

---

[30] "The racing incident is very loosely joined up with the development of the plot, and could easily be removed. The only connecting link is that one of Nana's many passing admirers is ruined through the exposure of the swindle. The other link connecting this episode with the main theme is even less substantial, and has nothing to do with the plot—and is for this very reason the more characteristic of Zola's style. The winning horse also bears the name Nana. And Zola makes the most of his opportunity to emphasize this coincidence. The victory of the courtesan Nana's namesake symbolizes her own triumphs in the Parisian beau monde and demi-monde." *Ibid.,* p. 96.

[31] "Thus the story of Vronsky's ride forms an essential part of the plot. Tolstoy emphasizes that this ride is not a mere episode, not an unimportant incident in Vronsky's life. The ambitious officer is hindered in his military career by a number of circumstances, among which his relations with Anna play a most important role. To win the race in the presence of the Imperial Court and high society is one of the few possibilities still remaining for the satisfaction of his ambitions. Thus, all the preparations for the race, all the phases of the race itself constitute parts of a very important act. They are related in their dramatic sequence. Vronsky's fall is the climax of this phase of his life; the fact that his rival outstrips him may be disposed of in one sentence." *Ibid.,* pp. 96–97.

[32] *Ibid.,* p. 97.

Zola's novels, according to these criteria, are riddled with contingency because of their author's insistent preoccupation with detail. Rather than leading away from itself to a central vision of reality, form becomes self-sufficient:

Zola describes the theater with his usual scrupulous completeness. First from the view point of the audience: everything that takes place in the auditorium, in the lobby, in the boxes, etc. The stage is described with extraordinary literary skill. But his tendency towards treatise-like completeness is not satisfied with that. He devotes another chapter of the novel to an equally elaborate dscription of the theater behind the scenes and as it looks from the stage. And in order to complete the picture, just as scrupulous and brilliant a description of a rehearsal is given in a third chapter.[33]

On the other hand, Balzac's portrayal of a theater scene in Les Illusions perdues utilizes only as much detail as is consistent with a realistic setting. The scene itself, like the horse race in Anna Karenina, constitutes an essential part of the plot development. Balzac's narrative style may be evaluated favorably because realistic detail effaces itself before the plot as a whole. Plot and description combine to form a narrative style which offers us a vision whose focal point lies beyond the aesthetic sphere. Accordingly, we find in Balzac a clear image of

the destiny of the theater under capitalism: the intricate and manifold subordination of the theater to capitalism and to journalism, which in its turn is subordinate to capitalism; the interrelation of the theater and literature, of journalism and literature; the capitalistic nature of the association of the life of actresses with open and secret prostitution.[34]

Zola's preoccupation with the means of presenting realism forces him to lose sight of the purpose for doing so. His self-contained descriptions, dialectically speaking, are static; they do not convey intentionality, or rather, they show us all too clearly that Zola's ideology does not have as its focal point the question "What is Man?" Thus, whereas "Balzac shows how the theater is prostituted under capitalism," Zola merely provides us with the information that may

---

[33] Ibid., p. 98.
[34] Ibid.

lead us, but will never oblige us, to see that capitalism prostitutes the theater.[35]

There seems little point in continuing the discussion. Intentionality for Lukács will always be judged according to the dialectical presupposition. As a result, formal analysis, like the study of literary character, constitutes another element in Lukács' dissociation of the author from his work. But the author's disappearance is only part of a more serious dissociation, that of the reader from his experience of the work.

The Lukácsian dialectic never sends us back to the literary object itself, but elicits our contemplation of a transformed object which has no correlative outside the critical dialectic itself, unless it is in the writings of those authorities responsible for the historical presupposition. To understand the radical subjectivity of Lukács' position, we need only attempt to focus first on the literary object and then on his criticism of it. A desire to demonstrate the historical and sociological implications of a work need not distort the patterns of meaning inherent in the work itself. Nevertheless, consideration of a literary object in terms of Lukács' description of it reveals little or no correspondence of real meaning. What we do find is a sensitivity, a feeling for historical and literary ideas. But in creating these evocative syntheses, Lukács has not focused on the object itself, but rather upon a reflection of the object, perception which he treats as though it were the object itself. In short, he confuses the perception with the perceived. Upon this "meta-object"—to borrow a fashionable prefix which he would quite rightly despise—Lukács erects what one of my colleagues has so appropriately called his *Begriffsdichtung*.

In conclusion, we might well ask whether the problems posed by Lukács' methodology are inherent in the concept of dialectical criticism, that is, criticism that seeks to move the reader to consider the literary object in specific, extra-aesthetic contexts. Must the dialectical critic abandon the hope of mediating between the reader and the

---

[35] "These social problems appear in Zola's novel also. But here they are described only as social facts, without exposing their origin. The theater director repeats incessantly: 'Don't say "theater"; say "brothel." ' Balzac *shows how* the theater is prostituted under capitalism. The drama of the central figures merges here with the drama of the establishment in which they are working, the things with which they live, the arena where they fight their battles, the surroundings among which their relationships find expression, through which they are materialized." *Ibid.*

literary work? Must he simply dictate what the work will represent and transform it accordingly?

The answer will inevitably depend upon the degree of tolerance one has for the consideration of literature in ethical rather than aesthetic terms. Granting the necessity to view literature as a means of obliging a reader to see the world in terms of current social and political problems, and the underlying human attitudes responsible for these problems, then Sartre must surely be considered. His attempt, in Qu'est-ce que la littérature, to elaborate a system of dialectical criticism must, one would think, be accepted as far more successful than Lukács'. If one cannot grant Sartre complete success—although he has been more successful than almost anyone else in this respect—one must at least grant that Sartre sets out to achieve his goal by the reverse procedure from that of Lukács. Rather than minimizing the points of contact between the reader and the literary object, he insists that reader and author stand in a special relation to one another and to the work. The work is the common bond, and its meaning the object of both author's and reader's concern. The critic becomes a temporary intruder in this relationship, a presence which must dissolve once the reader has taken upon himself full responsibility for his task as revealed by the writer. For the critic to erect his own perspective as a barrier between the reader and the work would not only be unthinkable, it would be self-defeating. Criticism, like literature, must not be conscious of itself, at least not to the extent of drawing attention away from the meaning of the work. The critical act, like the act of writing or reading, is based upon freedom, and it is freedom, not dialectical coercion, that ultimately guarantees their objectivity. Unfortunately, Lukács cannot trust his reader to make judicious use of his freedom. For Lukács, criticism is essentially parietal, and takes for its epigraph: in loco parentis lectori.

Dartmouth College

THE CRITICAL POSITION OF
ROLAND BARTHES

Hugh M. Davidson

A general review of the literary past has been going on in France since the Second World War, and with increasing momentum in the last ten years. The works have been approached in the light of new interests and inquiries. In the essays and books of Jean-Paul Sartre, Georges Poulet, Charles Mauron, Jean-Pierre Richard, Lucien Goldmann, and Jean Starobinski—to mention some of the leading names—one sees the results of this contact between the established works on the one hand, and on the other, principles coming from movements such as Marxism, Freudianism, existentialism, structuralism, and phenomenology. Actually there is little real consensus in this group of writers, although they refer to each other rather frequently. Their awareness of constituting a group seems to arise especially from the fact that they are reacting against the same things.

In the fall of 1965 Raymond Picard, a professor at the Sorbonne, and well-known for his exhaustive research—basically historical in conception—on Racine, published a short but hard-hitting little book entitled *Nouvelle critique ou nouvelle imposture (New Criticism or New Imposture)*.[1] While it is clear that Picard intended to question the procedures of the whole group of New Critics, his principal target was Roland Barthes, a professor at the *Ecole pratique des hautes études*, who had been indiscreet enough to publish in 1963 a volume of studies on Racine, done in one of the new modes. Barthes takes there, as his point of departure, the proposition that Racine's characters form a horde or tribe of about fifty people, dominated by harsh father-figures usually at war with their sons over women and power.

---

[1] Utrecht, 1965.

Picard was not at all convinced by this mixture of anthropology and psychoanalysis. By the time his rebuttal was finished, he had attacked Barthes for subjectivity, for violating the elementary rules of scientific thought (or, for that matter, of articulate thought), for cynical and obsessive preoccupation with sexuality, unverifiability, ambiguity, contradictions, aberrant extrapolations, jargon, inaccuracy, incoherence, arbitrariness, ideological impressionism, dogmatic fantasy, ignorance of recent scholarship, galloping systematization, and so on.

In February of 1966 M. Barthes gave his formal riposte, entitled *Critique et vérité*.[2] Some of his compliments, if less luxuriant, are hardly less deadly: Picard represents the interests of an intellectual caste; he speaks and defends the critical language not even of yesterday but of the day before yesterday; he is attached to phantasmic models of thinking and to a number of tautologies, linguistic myths, and stereotypes; and as his supreme weakness, he suffers from *asymbolia*, or more concretely, deafness to symbols. Noting the very generally favorable reception that had been given to Picard's attack, Barthes concluded that he had upset something quite deep-seated. The reaction of Picard and of those who agreed with him suggested, he said, that of an archaic community carrying out a rite of exclusion on a subject identified as dangerous. But there is much more to his reply. He states it in comprehensive terms, with interesting and effective distinctions; and so I believe it useful to present first a quick view of the whole situation as *he* sees it. After this survey of his exclusions we can turn, perhaps more easily than we otherwise could do, to the essential points of his critical position. For the most part, I shall follow the argument as Barthes has expressed it in *Critique et vérité*, with some added theses and ideas from *Sur Racine*, from *Mythologies* (1957) and from his volume of *Essais critiques* (1964).

On the one hand Barthes evokes the hostile camp of university criticism—*la critique universitaire*—with Raymond Picard, of course, as one of its most distinguished representatives. University criticism suffers, according to Barthes, from a usually unavowed positivism or concern with little facts, to the neglect of the spirit and symbolism of literature. It makes use of an outmoded set of psychological notions that go back to the 1880's. It also suffers from deterministic prejudices, for it insists on going inside the work to some alleged cause instead of exploring the domain that lies within it. The head or father-figure of this line of critics is, as we might expect, Gustave Lanson.

---

[2] Paris, 1966.

But, says Roland Barthes, Marx, Freud, and Nietzsche have been; "Il y a eu Marx, Freud, Nietzsche"; and some things have now to be redone.

In general opposition to this *critique universitaire*, Barthes sets up another type of criticism, one that he has described with various adjectives. Perhaps the most satisfactory one is contained in his phrase *critique idéologique*. He marks off thus a rough grouping, composed of people who, in their discussion of literature, use one of the principal intellectual languages now being spoken, who find their vocabulary and grammar, so to say, in Marxism, psychoanalysis, structuralism, existentialism, or phenomenology. (As a matter of fact, university criticism is a *critique idéologique*, without realizing it; it just happens to be the ideology of two or three generations ago.)

Within this group of so-called ideological critics, Barthes makes a distinction which seems to me to be of first importance. Goldmann, in his Marxist studies of Pascal and Racine, and Mauron, in his psychocritical studies of Mallarmé and Racine, seem to Barthes to have referred the works in each case to something external: right-wing Jansenism (Goldmann) or the psyche of the two poets (Mauron). Poulet, with his studies of human time and other basic themes, and Richard, with his thematic study of Mallarmé's work, bring a new kind of criticism into view: it is completely or almost completely immanent; it is a criticism of interpretation. Instead of explaining the work, or explaining it away, Poulet and Richard make it explicit, revealing its themes and variations, its coherence in terms of axiomatic ideas and obsessive images, its relation to an implied existential project.

At this point we reach the central views of Barthes, for a particular type of this *critique d'interprétation* is what interests him most. Let me begin by noting that Barthes admires linguistics, especially the structural kind. We are not surprised, therefore, to find that the reality he turns to at the start—the logical start, I mean—of his own reflection is *language*. To know literature one must first know language, since the former grows as a sort of parasite-system on the principal system formed by the latter. The truth of this proposition has become quite clear in the last hundred years, he thinks. From Mallarmé to Blanchot, writers have constantly recognized that language is the very matter of literature (*Critique et vérité*, p. 38).

Once decided upon, this step, this assimilation of literature to language, affects everything else. The literary work is not a thing, or more precisely, language transformed into a kind of object, as it is for some of our formalists in this country. Nor is it, while using language, essentially a kind of mental activity, like the peculiarly tight species of dialectical thinking that fascinates Poulet and that he finds everywhere he looks, or, again, like the concrete workings of sense and imagination that fascinate Richard, for whom the literary work is a key to the writer's encounter with the world. I realize that these formulas need to be qualified; I don't mean to exclude dosages of other and balancing ideas. But, with reservations stated and duly emphasized, it is still obvious that Barthes does not see in the work primarily an art-object or an act of knowing or feeling. It is significant language; it is a special kind of sign.

"Significant" and "sign" are important words here. Barthes borrows from de Saussure the distinction of *signifiant-signifié-signe*, the first referring to the vehicle, the second to what is conveyed, and the third to what comes into being through the association of the other two. By a special twist given to the notion of the *signifié*, what is signified, Barthes establishes the specific order of literary language. When language is involved in *praxis*, in activity designed to modify a situation, it is transitive, aimed at something beyond itself, and, indeed, limited in what it signifies by the situation to be changed. The tendency of language to ambiguity is thus checked by the circumstances. But literary language is intransitive; it covers or parallels the real world, but has no direct connection with it. There is no external situation surrounding literary language and restricting its semantic possibilities. As a result, such language becomes symbolic, that is, capable of sustaining more than one sense. It is enigmatic, like an oracle, and the critic composes, rather than recovers, the sense of it with the aid of vital elements present in *his* situation.[3]

By bringing thus into opposition unambiguous, practical, transitive language and ambiguous, impractical, intransitive, symbolic language, Barthes is able to isolate almost completely his object of study: a special kind of sign and process of signification. He criticizes the

---

[3] At the symposium on "The Languages of Criticism and the Sciences of Man," held at Johns Hopkins in October 1966, Barthes read a paper entitled "Ecrire: verbe intransitif?" in which it was clear that his views had evolved somewhat. He used the grammatical notion of diathesis or voice, specifically of the middle voice, to illuminate the activity of writing. In the middle voice, the agent or subject affects himself; transitivity is not excluded; the subject poses himself as contemporary with the writing, "being effected and affected by it."

"aesthetic" notion of the specificity of literature, dear to the Old Critics, who are satisfied by a tautology—"literature is literature." The specificity he has in mind is postulated, he says, within a general theory of signs that requires an understanding of logic, history, and psychology, or in short, a grasp of anthropology.

From the way in which he defines signification in literature, one can understand why he frequently insists on the fact—for him—that literature is essentially unrealistic (*irréaliste*). A writer eliminates almost entirely the denotative aspect of language; he exploits, instead, its connotative power. After all, Proust found a whole world in a single word—Guermantes. A writer is someone for whom *the* problem is language as a milieu having such depth and power. Language as an instrument, even as a decorated instrument, does not concern him. The general effect of this step—the isolation of literary language—is comparable, it seems to me, to that of the reasoning whereby Aristotle separates by attention to their origins, forms, and finalities art objects from other (natural or chance) things; or to that whereby Kant separates the perception and judgment of beauty and the sublime from other forms of mental activity. I think that one should add, however, that Barthes' distinction seems less radical than the other two, since it posits a continuous semantic line, bounded by a univocal sign at one end and a polyvalent symbol at the other, and both extremes may be found to some degree at every point on that line; whereas the distinctions of Aristotle and Kant presuppose discontinuities, metaphysical in the one case, critical in the other.

Where we are going can be indicated in another way if we return for a moment to Raymond Picard. As Picard has said in an interview, he believes in the notion of a recoverable historical sense for a work and for the language in which it is written. He further conceives of this sense as a function of a period or moment in the history of a civilization. If, after this task of recovery and referral—and the effort of self-denial implied in it—the critic wishes to see the relevance of the sense to his own time, he is free to do so. But as far as Barthes is concerned, excessive preoccupation with the historical and, for him, literal· sense reveals that *asymbolia* and critical deafness that I mentioned earlier.

This brings us to the heart of Barthes' position and to a statement of what the critic is supposed to do. For a given work, no one sense may be set up as a canon. Here are a few lines from an important passage:

La définition même de l'oeuvre change: elle n'est plus un fait historique, elle devient un fait anthropologique, puisque aucune histoire ne l'épuise. La variété des sens ne relève donc pas d'une vue relativiste sur les moeurs humaines; elle désigne, non un penchant de la société à l'erreur, mais une disposition de l'oeuvre à l'ouverture; l'oeuvre détient en même temps plusieurs sens, par structure, non par infirmité de ceux qui la lisent.[4]

Whatever societies may think or decree, he says, the work goes beyond them, goes through them, like an empty form that is filled successively by senses "more or less contingent and historical." Or, again, it is a sign with a sense that is both *posé et déçu*, offered and withdrawn (Barthes emphasizes the etymological meaning of *déçu*); it appears to answer a question while in fact merely asking it. The answer must be furnished by the reader or critic out of his own history, language, and freedom. Thus liberated from its scientific pretensions, criticism aims to tell us the sense that modern man can give to the works of the past. When it succeeds, the past is indebted to the present, and one can plausibly say that Racine owes something to Georges Poulet, as Verlaine does to Jean-Pierre Richard. "The work proposes, man disposes" (p. 52).

In fact, and it is essential not to miss this point, the critic does something that is consubstantial with what the writer did. To make a second writing with the first writing of the work: such is his task, according to Barthes (p. 14). One implication of this is that the sense elaborated by the critic must respect the symbolic character of the literary language: symbol must seek symbol (p. 73). As the work was written, so must he read and write. The need to harmonize the language of the work and the language of the critic follows on the recent change in the relationship of criticism to literature. Since Mallarmé the two functions—poetic and critical—of writing have tended toward exchange, interpenetration, solidarity. The reflexive meta-language of criticism accompanies and extends creative activity, so that now there is only one kind of writing (p. 46).

---

[4] "The very definition of the work changes: it is no longer an historical fact; it becomes an anthropological fact, since no history exhausts it. The variety of senses does not depend on a relativistic view of human customs; it designates, not an inclination of society to error, but a disposition of the work to openness; the work possesses at one and the same time several senses for reasons of structure, not because of weakness on the part of those who read it" (p. 50).

In *Critique et vérité* Barthes replies to one objection that is frequently addressed to him: that his conception of criticism leads fatally to subjectivity in interpretation. He lists three sanctions that apply to criticism as he understands it. (1) It must take everything into account; it must find a place in a system of meanings for every detail. (2) It must proceed according to definite rules; however, they will be derived, not from a model of scientific reasoning in the usual sense, but from the logic (as yet only partly developed and understood) of symbolic language. Here linguistics will be powerfully aided by psychoanalysis, which already can provide some of the formulas by which polyvalent language may be unified—either from the analysis of persons, as practiced by Freud and others, or from the analysis of substances, as exemplified in the works of Gaston Bachelard and his disciples. Barthes mentions specifically the processes of substitution, omission, condensation, displacement, denegation. (3) It must move always in the same direction, assuming the same conditions accepted by the writer, and, in particular, this basic one, that *language*, not the *person speaking*, is the subject under consideration. If these three sanctions are observed, the critic is not by any means free to say *n'importe quoi*. Bound by a kind of objectivity that fits his inquiry, he will trace out in a work long chains of transformations, developments of themes, and series of images.

Actually, criticism is only one of three activities that Barthes sees developing about literary works. It stands rather like a middle term between two other acts or disciplines. At the bottom, we have *lecture* or reading. When a text is merely read, the reader does not undertake to surround the original text or speech with a second text or speech; he desires the work, not his own language, as a means of doubling that of the author. On the second degree of the scale the critic accepts just this challenge, along with its risks, as he writes out the sense that he can give to the work. In the third place, Barthes sees the possibility of a science of literature, of a discipline that concerns itself not with the particular senses of literary works, but with their plurality of senses as a significant fact in itself, and with the logic of symbolic language. The model for this science is drawn from linguistics, specifically, from generative grammar. Just as generative grammar sets down the axioms, elements, and rules of combination for the construction of sentences in a language, so this science will state axioms, elements, and rules of combination for the construction of works, which are in a way like long and complicated sentences. Just as it is the business of such a grammar to state what the basis of *grammaticality* is in a language, so it will be the business of the science of literature to describe the conditions of *acceptability* in combinations of symbolic speech. In a way this ambitious program picks up where Mallarmé and Valéry left off; I see in it the same enthusiasm for elements, functions, and rules of composition, but raised to a more abstract and systematic level of treatment.

As I have presented it, we can begin to understand the critical position of Roland Barthes by paying attention to four things he does: (1) he places literature in the general context of language rather than of things or of thoughts; (2) he identifies it specifically as the intransitive and symbolic use of language; (3) he assigns to the critic the task of giving *a* sense, not *the* sense, to the work, realizing as he does so that other senses will be found as rivals to his own and that all senses are subject to replacement; (4) he integrates criticism into a scheme that includes the unexpressed gift of sense to a text, which is reading, and the study of polyvalent language, which is the science of literature.

The essays, short articles, and books in which Barthes develops these points introduce us to some of the most characteristic concerns of the *nouvelle critique* in France.[5] In one place Barthes tells us that the movement is national in character, with little or no debt to Anglo-Saxon criticism, to Spitzerism, or to Croceanism. I shall take this remark as the point of departure for a comment or two. During—let us say—the last thirty years the nature and history of literary criticism have been carefully explored here and in England. This exploration has made possible for us a new awareness of the types and limits of literary criticism, some discernment of the patterns involved in the frequent changes of alliance and fortune that seem to be its lot, and some understanding of the philosophic bases that underlie persistent differences of approach. In the light of this experience it would seem that the controversy over the *nouvelle critique* need not last very long, in this country at least. Is it legitimate to study literature as these new critics do? The only answer possible is, *Yes, of course.* Must everyone do this kind of thing? *No, of course not.* With these answers in mind, we can turn our attention from blank clashes of principle to results and to standards of performance. Those who decide to follow a different

---

[5] For a survey and further information, see Laurent LeSage, *French New Criticism* (University Park, Pa., 1967); for a vigorous discussion of the main points of view, see Serge Doubrovsky, *Pourquoi la nouvelle critique: critique et objectivité* (Paris, 1966).

line of thought—a non-dialectical line, for example—in connection with literature can surely learn from those who practice well another mode of criticism—and vice versa.

One further remark. It is impossible to miss the resemblances between what is being said in France and some of the discussions we had and heard in the period from about 1935 to 1960. There is the taste for immanent (we said "intrinsic") values in literature; there is the hostility to literary history, the tendency to oversimplify and caricature it, with the answering strong reactions from the representatives of that discipline; the decision to ask many of the important questions in terms drawn from linguistics and semantics, with some revival of interest in ancient rhetoric and poetics; the effort to distinguish literary language from other uses of language (we usually favored the negative analogies with science; Barthes prefers to say that literary language has nothing to do with *praxis*); the inclination to turn to the inventors of techniques for exploring pre- or extra-logical forms of thought (we had Frazer, Freud, and Jung; Barthes has Lévi-Strauss, Lacan, and Bachelard).

However, I prefer to end this exposition, which is too short to be adequate, by emphasizing some of the promises and hopes to be seen in Barthes' position. Thanks to its broad initial intuitions, it opens up the whole of literature as a great repertory of significant forms. It brings together in a way that has obviously the power to mobilize intellectual energies in France (and perhaps here), principles from psychoanalysis, for studying the psychic dynamism that pervades the content of literature; principles from linguistics, for the derivation of models both in critical procedures and in the literary science-to-be; and principles from anthropology, for the means of getting an exact perspective on history, and for models again, but this time, of typical human figures confronting one another and nature. Finally, it places before the critic a high ideal of technique, awareness of self, and sensitivity to contemporary problems.

Let us give the last word to Roland Barthes. Here is what he says in *Critique et vérité* about the results and aims of the new school:

Des livres critiques sont donc nés, s'offrant à la lecture selon les mêmes voies que l'oeuvre proprement littéraire, bien que leurs auteurs ne soient, par statut, que des critiques, et non des écrivains. Si la critique nouvelle a quelque réalité, elle est là: non dans l'unité de ses méthodes, encore moins dans le snobisme qui, dit-on commodément, la soutient, mais dans la solitude de l'acte critique, affirmé désormais, loin des alibis de la science ou des institutions, comme un acte de pleine écriture. Autrefois séparés par le mythe usé du "*superbe créateur et de l'humble serviteur, tous deux néces-saires, chacun à leur place, etc.,*" l'écrivain et le critique se rejoignent dans la même condition difficile, face au même objet: le langage.[6]

The Ohio State University

---

[6] "Certain books of criticism have, then, come into existence, offering themselves to be read in the same ways as works that are literary, properly speaking, although the authors of these books are, as to official status, only critics and not writers. If the new criticism has some reality, it is there: not in the unity of its methods, even less in the snobbism, which—it is convenient to say—sustains it, but in the solitude of the critical act, affirmed henceforth, far from the alibis of science or of institutions, as a deliberate act of *writing* in the full sense of that word (*un acte de pleine écriture*). Formerly separated by the worn-out myth of the 'proud creator and the humble servant, both necessary, with each in his place, etc.,' the writer and the critic now meet in the same difficult situation, facing the same object: language" (p. 46).

THE CRITIC AND EXISTENCE: AN
INTRODUCTION TO MENNO TER BRAAK

E. M. Beekman

At a time when the study of literature is in the process of becoming increasingly cosmopolitan, it is surprising that major literary areas are still virtually unknown. One such *terra incognita* is Dutch literature, particularly modern. The accusation that Dutch literature is a provincial subdivision of German lacks proof, for as any tourist can testify, Holland is probably one of the most cosmopolitan of continental societies. The First World War forced Dutch art to look beyond its borders; though Holland as a nation was at that time not physically violated, the conflict replaced an introverted with an international consciousness, a process that was not congenial to the traditions of the middle class, nor to the literary establishment. During the 'twenties three men vigorously attacked this bulwark, intent on setting the artist free from rigid aestheticism. In Flanders Paul van Ostaijen (1898–1928) single-handedly changed the artistic perspective of his generation, while in Holland Edgar Du Perron (1899–1940) and Menno Ter Braak (1902–1940) once and for all set a European standard for Dutch artists.

Ter Braak was born into the prosperous middle-class family of a physician in the town of Eibergen (province of Gelderland). He received his primary education there and went on to the *Gymnasium* in Tiel, a relatively large city in the same province. During these school years he suffered from a physical inferiority in what was primarily a rural society. At first he was able to maintain a status quo as the son of the town's physician, but he soon learned that his superior intelligence was less respected than physical prowess. As a youth he thought that, once he had reached the more intellectual level of the *Gymnasium* in Tiel, the problem would be solved. It was a great disappointment to him when he saw that there, too, muscular power and athletic excellence were the common denominators of a boy's life. "One was judged according to one's worth as a sportsman; and as a sportsman I was worth very little."[1] Yet at the same time, he confessed having been equally disgusted by his own type: "I was worth very little indeed, and I was forced to make friends with those for whom I myself very often felt contempt because they were pale, shy, bespec-tacled outcasts, disliked and pestered by the really sublime ones; I felt contempt and hated them in myself, I felt humiliated when I was walking with them and met the really sublime ones, the athletic gods. I was already old enough to try to console myself with the privilege of intellect (my intelligence for example); but it did not matter, I knew I was an outcast, inexorably . . ." (III, 120). Being an outcast he rel-ished the inversion of hierarchy during the last two years of the cur-riculum when mental qualities became the requirements for success: "They meekly began to listen to words, theories, and problems; they not only tolerated mental ascendancy, but accepted it as readily as if they had been waiting for it" (III, 120).

This triumph made him consider a theological career, as the Dutch critic H. A. Gomperts has suggested.[2] But by the time Ter Braak went to the University of Amsterdam, he had already been dis-illusioned by religion and followed a program of studies in history and Dutch literature. He became editor of a student periodical, *Propria Cures*, and showed the first evidence of his polemic ability in articles directed against a religious student organization. His public career began with contributions to the periodical *De Vrije Bladen (Free Pages)*, while he indulged his artistic interests in forming the *Film-liga*, a group of intellectual aesthetes devoted to cinematography.[3] After a short stay in Berlin for research, he earned his doctor's degree (*cum laude*) in 1928 with the dissertation *Kaiser Otto III; Ideal und Praxis im frühen Mittelalter (Emperor Otto III; Ideality and Reality in the Early Middle Ages*, I, 401–609), a work that deals with the attempt by Emperor Otto III (980–1002) to establish the spiritual ideal of St. Augustine's *De Civitate Dei* within the political context of the first century. Though a purely scholarly work, the theme is important for Ter Braak's future writings in that it juxtaposes an irra-tional dream (God's universal domain) with the historical reality of a political *terrena civitas*. This unresolvable duality is also the theme,

---

[1] *Verzameld Werk* (Amsterdam, 1950–51), III, 120. The edition, cited throughout, is in seven volumes. All translations are mine.

[2] *De Schok der Herkenning* (Amsterdam, 1959), p. 112.

[3] See the essays "Cinema Militans" and "De Absolute Film" in Vol. II.

to an extent, of *Carnaval der Burgers* (*The Burghers' Carnival*), while Ter Braak's detailed analysis of Augustinian thought forms the basis of his later book, *Van Oude en Nieuwe Christenen* (*Of Old and New Christians*). Having finished his education, Ter Braak taught for several years in Amsterdam and Rotterdam.

The *Burghers' Carnival* (1930), the first of Ter Braak's four great essays, is a lyrical dialectic on the fluidity of the becoming *I* as opposed to the abstraction of the calcified *We*. The poet is seen as the individual, the dreamer, the licentious element in life and in conflict with the communal burgher of solid traditions, morality, and materialism. Yet the poet is hidden in every burgher and the burgher is inevitable in every poet. In the intoxication of the carnival season (a metaphor for the absence of cultural inhibitions), these opposites briefly mingle in uncurbed freedom. But on Ash Wednesday sobriety returns and along with it the former polarities. In this and the following essay, *Démasqué der Schoonheid* (*The Unmasking of Beauty*, 1932), one finds the clearest statement of Ter Braak's conception of art. For him art can no longer be separate from the totality of existence which is both its origin and its mask. *Carnival* is a defense of the poet and of beauty, yet it opposes the notion of the poet as Olympian as well as the ideal of isolated beauty. The poet's creativity, Ter Braak argues, should no longer be judged solely by a conclave of specialists, but must be able to withstand a confrontation with existence. One must never forget, however, that Ter Braak, in attacking these ideas, intended not to discredit them but rather to redefine them.

According to the paradoxical structure of the argument, Ter Braak insists that, despite its sanctity, beauty must be known materially. "One desires to know the poet in the same way one knows the burgher: as the proprietor of his poem; one desires to know beauty as an immaterial matter, a distant gold from Ophir, which is hidden somewhere and which will sometime be found by the enterprising adventurers of the spirit. Even the dream does not escape the groping hands of the burgher" (I, 109). This passage indicates that beauty is not meant to be abstracted from reality, but that it should be ever present in concrete existence. Beauty and existence are part of a magnetic field of repulsion and attraction, shaping and destroying each other in perpetual becoming. Beauty becomes an undefinable presence of "everything which our abstractions are incapable of apprehending" (I, 117). One cannot say that it is either this or that, but only that it can be experienced in the act of creation. Unfortunately, at the same time that the act of creation knows beauty, it also materializes it (i.e., the poem) and beauty no longer reveals its true nature. The poem is a product, a possession, and this urge to possess represents the burgher in the poet:

The "difference" between the burgher and the poet is a carnival-difference. The poet, the professional poet, the one who produces, is a burgher, since he propagates, secures himself, maintains himself in his product. This product . . . has all the earmarks of the burgher's urge for possession; why should one deny it? It is a structure of commonplaces, color, line, sound, words, of elements and abstractions which every burgher can understand with his mind and can consequently either approve or reject.[4]

As one may surmise, it is difficult to determine precisely what constitutes Ter Braak's own conception of beauty, and one can only conclude that it may be described but not defined. It seems to be the experience of that one, strange moment during which a world, one's totality of existence, is suddenly illumined without grammatical finality: "For the discovery of things which causes a paralyzing happiness was . . . not given in proffered moments of a programmatically ordered beauty, but in seconds which vanish" (I, 109).

In Carnival Ter Braak was still in the camp of the poets and was injured by, rather than critical of, his environment. This Platonic discrepancy between reality and an ideal world is represented by the Christian symbolism of the fall of man. The poet is regarded implicitly as the ideal image of man and the burgher as the "fallen poet." The "carnival" (of life) symbolizes the fall from an irretrievably lost paradise: "This is our fall: we can no longer be pure poets, we have been denied paradise; we only celebrate the carnival of the burghers, which is already poisoned with Ash Wednesday; and the poets who write our verse always remain burghers who try in vain to escape from their burgher-grammar" (I, 31). The carnival, therefore, is "a lost para-

---

[4] I, 130. Commenting on the artist-burgher dialectic of the essay, the poet Hendrik Marsman suggested a correlation with Thomas Mann which he never pursued (Verzameld Werk [Amsterdam, 1960], p. 689). It seems to me, particularly in the case of Tonio Kröger, that Mann was equally critical of both the artist and the burgher. Lisaweta Iwanowna has to point out to Tonio that he is also partly a burgher, though towards the end of the novella he realizes that as an artist he remains more than a burgher and forever different (Meistererzählungen [Zürich, 1945], p. 131). Ter Braak's conclusion has its parallel in Tonio's insistence that one does not "dare [to] pluck even a single leaf from the laurel tree of art, without paying for it with one's life" (I, 130). Existence is the only totality.

dise which lives in our memory and which we can never hope to conquer again; forever discarding our forms, never released from the limitations of the forms, the burghers are forced to wander with the likeness of the lost poet in them, beyond recall and yet very close" (I, 31).

Actually, the essay has a fugal structure. The first chapter establishes the theme with its dialectical nature, which is pursued through six counterpoints (the "carnivals" of the children, the lovers, the devout, the burghers, and the poets) back to a reiteration of the theme in a final chapter on carnival morality. The language is poetic and baroque; it reflects the dialectic of the thesis in oscillating rhythms that give the book its aura of perpetual duration. The thought is subtly analytical—aphoristic at times—but mostly so dependent on formulation that form and content appear inseparable. Unlike any other of Ter Braak's works, Carnival is more lyrical than critical, more descriptive than analytical, and presents a discernible formal structure instead of seemingly diffuse monologues.

In 1930 Ter Braak was subjected to two important influences; he met Edgar Du Perron, with whom he formed a lifelong friendship, and less than a month later he discovered Nietzsche. In The Unmasking of Beauty, published two years after this decisive year, one finds a new Ter Braak: polemical, aggressive, purposely subjective in style. Yet Ter Braak was and remained an intellectual whose academic training was based on German and not on French thought. His inherent militancy was always checked by the intellectual's demand for truth and belief in the relativity of values. Therefore he would always allow his opponent a measure of validity; when he attacked he always managed to restore a great deal in the process of critical examination. In Carnival his style is that of an intellectual who has not yet purged himself of artistic aspirations. His latent wish for a more natural, subjective mode of expression, a greater militancy, and a more clearly defined criticism of cultural abstractions, he found embodied in the person of Edgar Du Perron. Marsman drew the following sketch of the Du Perron Ter Braak met in 1930:

Here was someone for whom the problem German metaphysics and French psychology did not exist; a man so un-German that he read Nietzsche in French: an a-religious, totally earthy nature, trained in the school of the French polemicists, who supported and defended his views with indefatigable tenacity. Du Perron was also in many ways a totally different figure from Ter Braak—much more romantic to begin with, and also much grimmer; much less Dutch, less social and less relativistic, really still the picture of the eighteenth century, non-conformistic *frondeur*.[5]

Du Perron was undoubtedly more limited in his thought, more artistic than intellectual. But this very limitation endowed him with polemical power. Stendhal's *"style trop haché"* was Du Perron's ideal; he shared the French writer's dislike for pretentious and verbose language. Thus it was under the influence of Du Perron that Ter Braak began to formulate and practice his theory of the "normal word." Furthermore, Du Perron allowed no quarter in literary combat and refused to admit to the relativity of values and intellectual positions. Ter Braak was as yet less dogmatic; he needed to be "liberated" from his excessive caution and from the intellectual's insistence on entertaining the validity of any given position. This happy confrontation with Du Perron served to draw out Ter Braak's hidden "second nature." Nor was this a one-sided relationship between two men who became known as the "Siamese twins." While Ter Braak gained a more forthright manner, Du Perron in turn acquired flexibility of thought and a sense of fair play.

In 1932 Ter Braak, Du Perron, and the Flemish writer Maurice Roelants (born 1895) started the periodical *Forum*, which lasted only three years. The first editorial (January 1932), written by Ter Braak, presents the view that became synonymous with the *Forum* generation:

We do not proclaim ourselves for or against poetry here, we only take sides against the deification of the form (the magic of "creation" as one is wont to call it in the Netherlands) at the expense of the creative being; we defend the notion that the personality is the first and last criterion in judging an artist. No matter what miracles take place during the process of creation: they appear to us only then important when the personality of the artist has been verified in his work. (IV, 269)

To counter critical provincialism, the mavericks of *Forum* renounced the arbitrary division between Dutch and Flemish literature and continued to discuss them as a single expression of the Dutch language with due regard to psychological, cultural, and political nuances. Furthermore, the members of the group refused to restrict themselves to national boundaries; they wanted to be "good Europeans" in Nietzsche's meaning of the phrase. Lastly, *Forum* warned the Dutch literary world of its polemical intentions:

---

[5] Marsman, *Verzameld Werk*, p. 694.

We will be polemical whenever we consider polemics to be necessary. Polemics are for us the self-infringement of the personality and we regard the fear of polemics, which tries to hide behind a careful and decent objectivity, as proof that those fearful ones do not know polemics as an affirmation of life, that they cannot conceive of polemics in any other way but as dispute. . . . A so-called constructive critique is a bloodless fiction; "the demand for constructive criticism is based upon the same false assumption that immutable truths exist in the arts, and that the artist will be improved by being made aware of them," says Mencken strikingly in his *Footnote on Criticism*. (IV, 269)

The proclamation attacked what Ter Braak and Du Perron felt to be the major affliction of Dutch culture and letters: *halve zachtheid*. This untranslatable expression denotes all dogmatic high priests of abstract doctrines—it describes those who would withdraw from a chaotic world behind the protection of institutionalized objectivity:

En prenant un ton très digne, en étalant des connaissances variées, en prodiguant des citations avantageuses, en se disant tendrement peinés des maux et des travers de notre monde moderne, ces publicistes usurpent une autorité que leur propre force d'âme et d'esprit ne leur aurait jamais procurée. Les jeunes écrivains dont il est question ici inventèrent pour ces faux sages le nom de "demi-doux," et ils ne manquent, maintenant encore, aucune occasion de les vitupérer.[6]

Forum wanted intellectual and moral honesty in the given reality of chaos and amorality. By reacting against formal aestheticism, it hoped to attract those writers who had found a "personal," i.e., subjective, mode of expression for themselves. These emphases were important enough to persist beyond the Second World War. What *Forum* stood for, and what its creators practiced, left a lasting impression on Dutch literary and intellectual life. It prepared the Dutch artist for the rapid changes of the contemporary world and dispelled from Holland's intellectual life a smothering nationalism.

The Unmasking of Beauty, Ter Braak's next major essay, shows the impact of these developments. For instance, it is here that Ter Braak begins his campaign for the total personality of the artist at the cost of traditional form. He now champions Stendhal and Nietzsche as "amateurs" who dare a "risk" of language (i.e., to write in a "natu-

---

[6] Johannes Tielrooy, *Panorama de la Littérature Hollandaise Contemporaine* (Paris, 1938), p. 161.

ral" style) without producing aesthetic "purity." Beginning with this work, Ter Braak's essays cease to be concise; the theme is woven into the exposition, in passages which circumscribe but do not define it. One can therefore only suggest the content of the book.

Generally speaking, *The Unmasking* discredits the sovereign beauty of the aesthetes by giving it psychological ambivalence. *Carnival's* opposition of poet and burgher becomes that of adolescent rebellion and sexagenarian dogmatism. Part One attacks abstract beauty in art by substituting personality for form; Part Two proposes the new critical norm of *le bon genre*, which includes writers like Stendhal and Nietzsche who understood the "greatest risk" of language. Such a view takes language as a dangerous medium and applauds as its best practitioners those writers who wage war for the "word" without adhering to "word-art" or a superimposed meaning. Ter Braak now demands a vigilant and sensitive probing for honesty in a writer's style; one should discipline oneself to obtain a fluidity of language and meaning akin to the ever changing reality of becoming existence.

The Unmasking of Beauty goes beyond *The Burghers' Carnival* in redefining the role and nature of the artist. Ter Braak admits the relative validity of the aesthetes' insistence on the hegemony of the senses. The significance of the aesthetes, as he sees it, is that they saved art from an "ethical censorship" that has little or no relevance to art at all:

What the aesthetes demand is nothing else but the claim of the senses. . . . They do not wish any interference from outside, no ethical censorship, no "comprehensibility-censorship" of the masses; they wish independence and autonomy for beauty, and in that they are perfectly correct. Ethical censorship is based on a cowardice which expects death and destruction from disinterested analysis, while the so-called "not-understanding" of modern art-products represents the typical form of snobbism in those who desperately do *not* want to be artistic snobs. (II, 598)

Nevertheless, at this point art has still not been made self-sufficient. Aestheticism has severed art from reality, thereby denying art its ultimate purpose, to point "back to contemptuous nature" (II, 595). Ter Braak proposes a reeducation of the artist which would lead him to what he calls the "third interpretation" of beauty:

Beauty leads the adolescent from nature to art since in art he can rebel more violently against nature; but it leads the poet just as surely back from art to nature, but only if he has still ample suppleness to leave art behind him. Then, if beauty finds art once more, it has lost the pride of the aesthetes—lost it to nature. This art is the third possibility. That third possibility is the unmasking of beauty in the new confrontation with nature, which also entails art. Beauty faces us again in her adolescent form as deliverance, as loss; her simple origin is rediscovered, the Delphic level has disappeared; one can now justify art without oracles and miracles. (II, 595)

One should notice again Ter Braak's persistent demand for an inclusive interpretation of both existence and art, and his continued attack on the tendency to attribute an "absolute importance" to things (II, 596). We saw this iconoclasm in *Carnival*, and we will rediscover it in subsequent works; indeed, it appears to be the central preoccupation of Ter Braak's work.

While dissecting aestheticism, Ter Braak did concede one positive element of the aesthetes' position: it had at least a subjective relationship to art. The objective critics, however, Ter Braak maintains, have no relationship to art whatsoever and yet they portentously claim to have the "correct method" for interpretation "in the hermetically closed domain of Beauty, since return to nature means for them the destruction of that domain wherein they became such excellent officials" (II, 599). For the objective critic, Ter Braak continues, the varieties of art have become a collection of isolated objects which are then judged with the presumption of infallibility. Ter Braak feels that this singular devotion of both aesthete and objective critic to the abstract product of art, comes from the fear of seeing the artist as an existential entity. One must suspect hierarchies of values and autonomous principles since nothing is absolute or isolated in the fluid relativity of the process of existence. In his belief in the precariousness of life and its essential absurdity, Ter Braak joins such modern artists as Brecht, Ionesco, and Dürrenmatt.

In 1933 Ter Braak stopped teaching in order to devote himself entirely to his criticism. He became literary editor of *Het Vaderland* (*The Nation*) and held this position until his death in 1940. He wrote a large number of so-called book reviews, actually thoughtful essays on continental literature and society. A good example of the longer pieces which he collected in book form, is the volume *In Gesprek met de Vorigen* (*Conversing with Precursors*, 1938), which discusses writers from Erasmus to Thomas Mann.[7]

---

[7] At this stage of his career, if not in his entire work, Ter Braak resembles Edmund Wilson. *Conversing with Precursors* and an earlier work, *Man tegen Man* (*Man against Man*, 1931), are akin to Wilson's *The Shores of Light* and

Politicus zonder Partij (Politician without Party, 1934) shows Ter Braak at the height of his powers. No longer does one find an exposition built around paradoxical principles which both include and reject each other as in *Carnival* or even *The Unmasking of Beauty. Politician without Party* is the actualization of *Forum's* credo: a "personality" with all its complexities discusses polemically a culture by constantly referring to that culture's impact on a subjective consciousness. The book also puts Ter Braak's theory of language into practice. Discarding a tradition of form, the book argues for the "natural" compulsion of formulating one's thought. It is Ter Braak's attempt at a critical confrontation with himself to seek intellectual honesty and moral clarity without making either one an end or a means in itself.

The first part of the book, entitled "The Writer after His Thirtieth Year," discusses the problem of language in general and Ter Braak's own style in particular:

I still know little more than that I write because I have to . . . which is the reason that I write in the digestive language of memoirs; for those who do not *need* to write and nevertheless do so because they happen to be used to the constant movement of their right hand, hide their digestion as something indecent. My style, therefore, does not become nonchalant; I wish to digest rhythmically. No one wants idealistic eructations, while the daily rhythm of digestion betrays more of someone's "interior" than he would admit to himself, and betrays exactly that which he is prone to hide behind a show-window of civilized products. The honesty and courage of digestion: that is what I want to vouch for. (III, 29)

It also explains that the first person singular is by no means the autobiographical *I* of confessional literature, but rather a polemical *I* which serves as a shield in the literary campaign against an entire culture. The chapter "History of an Intellect" traces the development and at the same time examines the content of what is commonly known as one's "intelligence." It becomes clear that Ter Braak's own intellectual history was essentially a confrontation with chaos in the course of a relentless pursuit of monolithic abstractions and cultural taboos. His honesty forced him to reexamine his own weapons and resulted

---

Classics and Commercials. Wilson's *The Triple Thinkers* and *To the Finland Station* could be compared to Ter Braak's *Of Old and New Christians* (1937), which is a critique of Marxism, Socialism, Fascism, and Nazism. An interesting coincidence is that both Ter Braak and Wilson wrote two novels which, as creative excursions, are considered inferior to their critical efforts.

in a semantic understanding of his own intelligence. Despite his intellectualism Ter Braak was able to look beyond himself to discover that intellect, too, can take the guise of being invincible and magical. In the fourth part, "Sinning against the Holy Ghost," he shows how dangerous intellect can be when it becomes a means for self-preservation. As was mentioned earlier, Ter Braak had only his superior intelligence to oppose the domination of brawn in his childhood. Now he readily admits to the former danger of intellectual *hybris* and castigates himself for his hatred of "the right of the strongest." "The intellectual feels a clammy disgust when he must witness scenes which do not fit into his scheme of things. Only now, free from former demands, have I succeeded in determining this disgust: it was the same hatred of physical superiority which made me as a child idolize the 'mental' teacher, it was the aversion of the right of the strongest which one always finds in weak, vindictive natures" (III, 123).

But Gomperts points out that "Ter Braak needed to mirror himself the truth of his youthful incentive to proclaim his mental superiority, wherein he saw a compensation for his failure in the physical realm of existence. That is to say, he desired to unmask theories as interests since the psychology of Nietzsche, with its reduction of everything to 'der Wille zur Macht,' had taken a hold of him. He was prepared to do so because of his Protestant inclination to examine his conscience, self-analysis, and through his habit taken from Hegelian philosophy, to see in all appearances their opposites. Before he encountered Nietzsche, he was still able to undermine his own spiritual basis. But the readiness to do so was there from the very beginning in a provisional form."[8] This particular confession has led to many speculations about Ter Braak's "traumatic" disgust with violence and explains, for some people, his suicide in 1940. The matter is not quite that simple, as I will explain shortly.

In the third part of *Politician without Party*, "Nietzsche versus Freud," Ter Braak records his intellectual encounter with the former. He compares Nietzsche to Freud in order to illuminate what precisely he admired in *his* interpretation of the German thinker. For Freud he admits an ambivalent admiration; he admires the discoveries of the Viennese doctor, his style, "his dislike of the philosophers, his cold disdain for the infantile illusions of Christianity, his preference for the 'biology of the mind' . . . three things which I consider to be unmistakable earmarks of an intelligent man, and which the less

---

[8] *De Schok der Herkenning*, p. 113.

chaste renegades Adler and Jung, therefore, tried to remove from the system . . ." (III, 77). But he found himself disliking Freud when he saw how these three "earmarks of an intelligent man" were nullified by Freud's blind devotion to his own system. "I saw the despiser of the religio-narcosis and the philosopher's idiom on his knees in front of the idol Science and, worse yet, in front of his own complex terminology: psychoanalysis" (III, 78).

In Nietzsche Ter Braak saw (to use Nietzsche's own phrase) a "friend." He admired his psychological subtlety, his total commitment to a controversial philosophy, and his highly subjective style which scorned all specialized jargon (III, 91). The thinker who denied importance to the consequences of his thought, the ironical aphorist, the poet who wrote philosophical essays and the philosopher who unmasked abstractions in a lyrical language—this was the man who captured Ter Braak's imagination. "Nietzsche was for me what Schopenhauer had been for Nietzsche; 'I understood him as if he had been writing for me'; the printer's ink and the difference in generations could not force the customary paralyzing isolation, because the punctuation marks still held the unintentional spontaneity of the writer who, having no concern for either vulgarity or poetry, had written for friends" (III, 89). Gomperts concludes his discussion of Ter Braak's encounter with Nietzsche with the admonition that "Nietzsche with the fluctuating truth, who was always ready to give his results away or laugh at them, was the extension of Ter Braak himself with his indomitable urge to unmask, to find in each concept its opposite and to experience all formulas as paradoxes."[9] "Ter Braak's friend whom he called Nietzsche, was in reality someone who resembled Nietzsche but who was Ter Braak."[10]

In the final section, Ter Braak introduces the concept of l'honnête homme, based on Pascal, whose description he quotes:

Universal individuals are called neither poets nor geometricians, etc.; but they are all that and at the same time judges of all those things. One does not deify them at all. It is necessary that one will not say either "he is a mathematician," or "preacher," or "eloquent," but "that he is an honest man." Only that universal quality pleases me. (III, 170)

This is Ter Braak's "party" with its platform of humanity and honnêteté. The concept was the impetus for his formulation of "human

---

[9] Ibid., p. 124.
[10] Ibid., p. 125.

dignity" in his last important essay, *Van Oude en Nieuwe Christenen*.

In 1937 when *Of Old and New Christians* was published, totalitarian ideologies had strengthened themselves in Europe and Ter Braak could no longer refrain from opposing them. In his new work he argued that European culture is a derivative of Christianity; despite prevailing irreligious tendencies, we are all inheritors of the Church of Christ. "Old Christianity" was most clearly formulated in St. Augustine's *De Civitate Dei*. To summarize the argument: the medieval theologian judged men's actions according to morality—when one's actions served the kingdom of God they were admirable, but if the same actions were for the benefit of Satan they were sinful. Such a distinction was legislated by the existence of a hereafter where good was rewarded and evil punished. Christianity's insistence on the equality of man before God was assured by the immortality of the soul and its just reward in Heaven. Ter Braak, however, believes that this notion camouflages the basic inequality of human society with the promise of heavenly equality and salvation. The concept of the Christian dignity of man, Ter Braak insists, is based on this promise of a spiritual equality which, he feels, originated in the "resentment" of the early Christians for their oppressors in the first century A.D.

This theory can be traced to Nietzsche's *Der Antichrist*, but whereas Nietzsche applies the theory specifically to democracy, Ter Braak sees its influence throughout European culture from St. Augustine to Hitler. When the belief in personal salvation and heavenly reward disappears, Ter Braak argues, the distinction between heavenly equality and earthly inequality is nullified unless a worldly ideology can provide a replica which would resemble the former belief in the hereafter. He finds that this basically Christian pattern persists in European history into the twentieth century. With the absence of a Christian heaven to insure human equality after death, Marxism fills the vacuum with the illusionary promise of a classless society in a nebulous future of the total victory over capitalism. The vulgar credo of National Socialism announces a contemporary realization of the hereafter in the superiority of one race, as soon as that race has gained complete control of the world. Marxism reflects resentment in its hatred of the bourgeois, while National Socialism practices nothing but hatred for anything not itself. Ter Braak goes on to postulate the theory that resentment is a lethal and yet kinetic force of European civilization. The only possible position left, so he feels, is to accept this as a *fait accompli*. He furthermore advocates a "new elite" of a democracy of "opportunism"; i.e., a democracy which has as its platform the *honnêteté* and dignity of a human being. Its "opportunism" consists of the ability to maneuver between prevalent ideologies with *l'honnêteté de l'homme* as only constant.

Ter Braak continued his political investigations even when it became clear that Hitler was rapidly becoming an international menace, and from 1937 until his death in 1940, Ter Braak attacked the dogma of Nazism relentlessly. He was one of the few who had studied, understood, and translated *Mein Kampf*. In 1937 he published the pamphlet *Het Nationaalsocialisme als Rancuneleer (National Socialism as the Doctrine of Rancor)*. He translated and wrote an introduction to Hermann Rauschning's book *The Nihilistic Revolution; Appearance and Reality in the Third Reich*, which was published in 1939, followed in 1940 by another work of Rauschning, *Hitler's Own Words; Political Conversations with Hitler Concerning his Real Intentions*. Ter Braak had come full circle: from the lyrical discourse on what is essentially a poetic image of great profundity (*Carnival*), the critic was now involved in "existence." For Ter Braak, existence and criticism were never really separate.

When the Nazis invaded Holland on May 10, 1940, Ter Braak realized that he was in grave danger, and rather than fleeing he chose to commit suicide. Many post-war critics have reduced his death to a psychological inevitability resulting from his "neurotic" fear of violence and the "right of the strongest." But Simon Vestdijk, one of Holland's most distinguished authors, gives a more reasonable explanation (Vestdijk began his career as a physician and had medical support for his opinion):

Despite the flexible intelligence which he used to guide and continually check himself, Ter Braak was nevertheless a neurotic personality; his tendency for depression during moments of extreme tension finally cost him his life. His suicide may not be ascribed to a whim. Several years before the war he consulted one of our leading psychiatrists who later told me that Ter Braak already at that time was determined to commit suicide if the Germans invaded Holland. This was a matter of principle with him. . . . Yet it still may have been the only solution. One does not see someone like Ter Braak either going into hiding or fleeing to England, though they appear now as the most logical choices; and the Germans, the first or second day at his doorstep, would certainly have tortured him to death (the involvement with Rauschning's books being in his case the principal crime).[11]

---

[11] Simon Vestdijk, "Gestalten tegenover mij," *Maatstaf*, VIII (November 1960), 492.

The same day Ter Braak committed suicide (May 14, 1940), Du Perron died of a heart attack. The poet Marsman drowned that June, when his ship, while crossing the Channel to England, was torpedoed by a German submarine.

The parallel between Ter Braak's thought and Kierkegaard's theory of "indirect communication" which seeks to destroy the illusion of abstractions has not been appreciated. In *Concluding Unscientific Postscript* Kierkegaard says that indirect communication can give no semblance of certainty since "certainty is impossible for anyone in the process of becoming":[12]

An existing individual is constantly in the process of becoming: the actual existing subjective thinker constantly reproduces this existential situation in his thoughts, and translates all his thinking into terms of process. It is with the subjective thinker as it is with a writer and his style; for he only has a style who never has anything finished, but moves "the waters of language" every time he begins, so that the most common expression comes into being for him with the freshness of a new birth.[13]

Such a manner of communication is "the art of taking away . . . when a man has much knowledge, and his knowledge has little or no significance for him, does a rational communication consist in giving him more knowledge, even supposing that he is loud in his insistence that this is what he needs, or does it not rather consist of taking some of it away?"[14] Kierkegaard's "indirect communication" mingles jest and seriousness. Its principal aim is to destroy a culture's illusions. One compels the reader to take notice, and in turn obliges him to judge. In order to bring someone who has lived most of his life under an illusion to the truth, one employs the "negative" to remove the illusion, and one "deceives" him into the truth.

Ter Braak never assumed finality for his work; he stressed the process of language: "The great risk: to remain music and not to flow into the narcosis of music. To seek always the formula and never to freeze into 'truth'" (III, 644). *The Burghers' Carnival* ends with the statement that "one must not be able to finish since it sobers a book—that formal and dignified burgher—with the semblance of completion, of totality, of leaving behind, or it induces a sleep of

---

[12] Søren Kierkegaard, *Concluding Unscientific Postscript* (Princeton, 1960), p. 311.

[13] *Ibid.*, p. 79.

[14] *Ibid.*, p. 245.

burgher-contentment, to have completed something. This paper
burgher, built from every type of word and constructed according to
a certain syntax, remains invitingly behind, waiting; waiting for
whom?" (I, 196). As to subjectivity of style, surely polemics is one of
the most subjective ways of writing. Indeed, one could call Kierkegaard's work a polemic against Hegelian philosophy and nineteenth-
century society, and similarly, one could summarize Ter Braak's
career as the process of unmasking. Constantly seeking the true nature
of abstractions by immersing them in the flow of life, Ter Braak
unmasks the poet in *The Burghers' Carnival*, the aesthete in *The
Unmasking of Beauty*, and the intellectual in *Politician without Party*,
and spends the last years of his life revealing the dangerous false-
hoods of political ideologies. To be sure, in the process of destroying illusions, Ter Braak did stress their negative qualities. As was
pointed out earlier, however, he did not discredit but redefined them
within the process of existence. As Kierkegaard puts it: "The true is
not higher than the good and the beautiful, but the true and the good
and the beautiful belong essentially to every human existence, and
are unified for an existing individual not in thought but in existence."[15]

Championing the poet against the plurality of the burghers in
Carnival, the iconoclastic writer against the aesthetes and the formalistic critics in *The Unmasking of Beauty*, and the lone *honnête
homme* against the profusion of political ideologists, Ter Braak
adhered consistently throughout his life to the doctrine of individuality—something which Kierkegaard found sadly wanting in his own
age. The following quotation from Kierkegaard's *Concluding Unscientific Postscript* not only reveals Ter Braak's central concern in his
work, but is also very much applicable to the present:

In the midst of all our exultation over the achievements of the age . . .
there sounds a note of poorly conceived contempt for the individual man;
in the midst of self-importance of the contemporary generation there is
revealed a sense of despair over being human. Everything must attach itself
so as to be part of some movement; men are determined to lose themselves
in the totality of things, in world-history, fascinated and deceived by a
magic witchery; no one wants to be an individual human being.[16]

The Dutch essayist is a perfect example of what Kierkegaard defined
as the ideal subjective thinker: "Every human being must be assumed

[15] *Ibid.*, p. 311.
[16] *Ibid.*, p. 317.

in essential possession of what essentially belongs to being a man. The task of the subjective thinker is to transform himself into an instrument that clearly and definitely expresses in existence whatever is essentially human."[17]

Ter Braak was the first critic to introduce Thomas Mann to the Dutch public, and Mann particularly remembered Ter Braak's essay on *Lotte in Weimar*, calling it "the finest, if I dare judge, which has as yet appeared, full of sagacity and sympathy, an ideal example of creative criticism." Recalling the many deaths of Dutch artists as a result of the Second World War, Mann ends with this homage:

Why does the loss of Ter Braak appear to me as the most bitter one? Because he was personally the closest to me? [Mann had met Ter Braak in 1939.] No, but rather because the creative critic is perhaps even rarer than the pure poet—and perhaps even more indispensable at this time. . . . Often did I have to think of him in the streets of Amsterdam, in The Hague and on these shores. At this time, being about to embark in the seriously wounded city of Erasmus for the return journey to my new fatherland, my farewell to Holland, to Europe, will be bound to an affirmation of my admiration for the good Dutchman, the good European Menno Ter Braak.[18]

University of Massachusetts

---

[17] *Ibid.*, p. 318.

[18] Thomas Mann, "In Memoriam Menno Ter Braak," in the commemorative collection of essays, *Over Menno Ter Braak* (Amsterdam, 1949), p. 8.

THE LITERARY CRITICISM OF
FRIEDRICH GUNDOLF

René Wellek

In June 1923, when I was not yet twenty, I attended, at Heidelberg, a single lecture by Friedrich Gundolf. A tall, darkly handsome man, standing in the light of the window, turned his profile with a strong nose self-consciously to the large audience filling the hall and recited, in a level monotone, a lecture that could have been printed, word for word, in any of his books. I now remember little except the aura of a solemn ceremony, and the worshipful attitude of the listeners. Later, in the afternoon, a visit to his house—on the strength of an introduction from Marianne Weber, the widow of Max Weber—revealed a more humane human being: a brilliant talker accustomed to the deference of his youngers. (He was then not quite 43 years of age.) Gundolf's occupancy of what, after Berlin, was the most prestigious chair of German literature—to which he was appointed in spite of his ostentatious contempt for footnotes, acknowledgments, polemics, and bibliographies—and the wide sale of his books: *Shakespeare und der deutsche Geist* (1911) and *Goethe* (1916) made him the representative figure of the victory of the new literary scholarship over that of the nineteenth century: its factualism, its dependence on external biography, its accumulation of filiations, parallels, sources and analogues, in short, the antiquarianism dominating the German (and not only the German) universities.

The year before I had entered the Czech University of Prague in order to study Germanic philology. I had soon been disillusioned by the training; I did not care for Gothic vocalism and consonantism, nor for the (anyhow largely fictional) biographies of dozens of Minnesängers nor for the sources of Grillparzer's *Libussa* nor even for the precise itinerary of the Nibelungen down the Danube to their doom.

Gundolf's books—free of pedantry, dazzling by the boldness of their generalizations and the authoritative tone of their judgments—seemed to hold up a new hope for what literary history could be or could become. But somehow I was subtly repelled by what I had seen at Heidelberg. I could not but feel that the implied demand for complete allegiance and even abject subservience to a creed was foreign to my nature. I gave up the idea of studying under Gundolf and soon shifted in Prague from Germanic philology to English literature where a sensible and concerned teacher, Vilém Mathesius (later the founder of the Prague Linguistic Circle), taught me to read Chaucer and Spenser and even H. G. Wells and Bernard Shaw.

I recall this day forty-five years ago not for any self-indulgence in autobiographical reminiscence but as an explanation of the peculiar mood with which I approached the rereading of Gundolf's writings after many years of neglect. I tried to evoke the fascination these writings had for me and many contemporaries and I tried to account for the fading of my interest which obviously has been shared by many other readers of my generation. Clearly it involves the general reaction against Gundolf's master, Stefan George, the deep suspicion with which he is viewed as a prophet of the Third Reich, though he himself went into voluntary exile under the Nazis and though Gundolf, as a Jew, would have suffered persecution from them if he had lived long enough. A good defense can be made against the accusations of Fascism or pre-Nazism hurled, for instance, by Georg Lukács at the circle with which he was himself loosely associated in his early years.

Still, there is no denying that the adoration and even adulation which exalted George not only to a great poet but to a prophet, leader, master, and even head of a spiritual "state" who imposed tasks on his disciples, banished them from his presence when they failed to meet his demands, and, in general, cultivated contempt for the public, was profoundly undemocratic. George must be seen in the context of late nineteenth-century aestheticism, in the company of Mallarmé and his aristocratic gestures, in the wake of Nietzsche and his exaltation of superman, and he must be put into the peculiar German context of a reaction against the shabby Philistinism of the Hohenzollern Empire, against the dominance of naturalism and the decline of poetry into inconsequential ornament or sentimental consolation.

George himself was hardly a literary critic, but the importance of his model and his, mainly oral, instruction in directing the change of literary taste and even the style and methods of the literary criticism of his followers must not be underrated. His scattered statements col-

lected in *Tage und Taten* (1903) suffice to bring out his basic attitude: the emphasis, at first at least, on art for art's sake and certainly
the purity of art inimical to daily politics, the worship of form and language, of poetic language set off by sound, diction, and even print and
paper from vulgar use; the exaltation of a few great poets of the past:
Dante, Shakespeare, and Goethe; the discovery of Hölderlin and the
rediscovery of Jean Paul; the introduction, in George's translations, of
Baudelaire, Mallarmé, Verlaine, and the Dutch Albert Verwey; the
harsh rejection of the nineteenth century, and of the whole romantic
tradition.

Surprisingly, George was able to attract and to inspire a group of
men who were or became scholars and critics. Of this group, Gundolf,
who met George when he was only nineteen, was to become the one
writer whose influence would be most profoundly felt in German
scholarship and literary criticism. Gundolf's book on George (1920)
was a late act of homage, extravagant in its adoration, which does not
even hint that pupil and master had come to a parting of the ways.
The published correspondence shows Gundolf's agonized squirmings
under the master's disapproval of his association with Elisabeth Salo-
mon, whom he was later to marry. But even to the day of his death
Gundolf lived under George's shadow: he kept the promise of his last
letter to George in 1926, announcing his marriage; "I shall not desert
you even though you reject me."[1]

Still, as a critic and literary historian, Gundolf developed his
method (if not his judgments and attitudes) independently of George.
He studied, after all, under Erich Schmidt at the University of Berlin
and published a fairly conventional thesis on *Caesar in German Literature* (1903): it anticipates the later book on *Caesar, the History of
His Fame* (1924), which centers around the concept of the "image,"
the "legend" of a great man, which was one of the overriding concerns
of the George-circle: a restitution of hero-worship, a belief in the
exemplary power of the great men in history.

Gundolf's first (and possibly his best) book of literary history,
Shakespeare und der deutsche Geist (1911), assumes also an almost
prescriptive power for Shakespeare in Germany. The whole history of
German literature from the seventeenth century to the Romantic
movement is conceived of as a struggle to approach Shakespeare: his

---

[1] Stefan George-Friedrich Gundolf: *Briefwechsel*, ed. Robert Boehringer
and Georg Peter Landmann (Munich, 1962), p. 372. For this and subsequent
references see the appended Bibliographical Note.

language, his poetry, his tragic or comic feeling, not only through translations and adaptations or critical estimates but in creative competition and in drama as well as in the lyric or the novel. The book combines, with amazing success, a close though highly selective look at the stylistic details of German translations and imitations of Shakespeare with sweeping generalizations about the progress of the German literary language and culture. The German language is conceived as originally incapable of adequately rendering Shakespeare. The incredibly crude versions of Shakespeare demonstrate the low state of comprehension in the seventeenth century; Shakespeare is then understood only as brute matter, external plot (Stoff); in the eighteenth century, with Lessing and Wieland, Shakespeare is at last appreciated as form (Form); while only with Herder and Goethe can one speak of a comprehension of Shakespeare as import, as meaning (Gehalt), as a totality. The neat triad of progression leads up to August Wilhelm Schlegel's version, which is praised as fully adequate. The poetic conquests of Goethe have lifted the German language to the level of Shakespeare.

Similarly the progress of German criticism of Shakespeare is traced in neat stages from enemies such as Gottsched, to apologists such as Elias Schlegel and Bodmer, to defenders (Lessing), panegyrists (Herder), and zealots such as the dramatists classed as "Storm and Stress." Epigrammatically, Gundolf formulates the contrast between Lessing and Herder: "Lessing justifies Shakespeare before the Greeks by saying: Shakespeare is also art, while Herder does the same, saying: The Greeks are also nature" (SudG, 203). One can object to details of the book. The almost uncritical acceptance of August Wilhelm Schlegel's translation surprises particularly as Gundolf spent years on a translation of his own which reproduced Shakespeare in a baroque, tortuous, bookish language often far removed from the polished, somewhat Schillerian performance of his predecessor. Nor can one quite sympathize with Gundolf's characterization of the German romantic movement which he sees as purely destructive, ironic, and uncreative. One may wonder at the contradiction between the allusion to Bergson (SudG, 58) and his sense of flux, the basic conception of history as a play of forces or a stream of tendencies rather than a row of books or even a sequel of persons with the almost playful dryness of some classifications and enumerations. Still, Gundolf produced a history of Shakespeare's influence in Germany which is also a cross section through German literature and thought of such convincing power of formulation and concrete observation that compared to it all older treatments seem mere accumulations of lifeless materials.

Shakespeare und der deutsche Geist did not, except in tone, break with the tradition of German *Geistesgeschichte*. It relies, too much to my mind, on the dualistic typologies of the German tradition emanating from Schiller's treatise on naive and sentimental poetry; on the contrasts between classical and romantic, Apollonian and Dionysiac art, the seesaw between form and movement, sculpture and music, "attracting" and "expansive" geniuses, synthesis and analysis or the antinomy of intellect and passion, reason and imagination, Rationalism and Irrationalism. Thus the book on *Goethe* (1916) means a radical break: it focuses on one person so exclusively that we hardly hear or feel anything of the history of the time or the history of literature before or around him.

Gundolf, in his *Goethe*, aims at a special kind of monograph: the evocation and construction of a "figure" (*Gestalt*) which is conceived as a union of life and work (G, 1). Gundolf rejects external biography (and tells us very little of it); he, rightly to my mind, sees the center of any literary study in the works of an author, while letters, diaries, and conversations at most serve as corroborating evidence. But he still does not want to write criticism in the usual sense of judging books. He sees the works as a form of life or, as he says in a Spinozistic formula, "Life and work are only diverse attributes of one and the same substance, of a spiritual-corporeal unity which appears as both form and movement simultaneously" (G, 1). This unity of being and becoming is, metaphorically, described as "a globe of forces" (G, 15) rather than a linear growth. Works are compared to "annual rings on a tree." Goethe, and implicitly every creative man, fulfills an inner necessity, a predetermined fate, an unalterable pattern. Works are thus written without any external aims (G, 14), compulsively, instinctively. The artist, we are told many times, experiences differently than an ordinary man (G, 2), in terms anticipating his work, and thus puts himself above and beyond any moralistic criticism. Gundolf, with almost comic solemnity, defends Goethe's desertion of Friederike Brion as a necessity of his nature, as a needed sacrifice to Goethe's future (G, 144–145). In constant variations we hear of Goethe's "inborn entelechy" (G, 14) and the "demonic unity or the mutual penetration of the inner and outer forces in his life" (G, 235).

Gundolf sees something predestined, fatal but also internally anticipated in Goethe meeting Herder or Charlotte von Stein. This leads him to such extravagancies as seeing Goethe's friends assembled around as his "own system of human types" (G, 211) or saying that he "composed the poems to Friederike not because he met her but he met her because these songs vibrated in him" (G, 58). The tone of adoration reaches heights of absurdity when Goethe is seriously referred to as "Zeus" (G, 741) and when the *Conversations with Eckermann* are called "not a printed textbook or a collected harvest of wisdom but a Gospel, i.e. the voice of a holy figure" (G, 746). The eminently human and even bourgeois figure of Goethe is raised on a pedestal so high that he disappears in a cloud of incense.

Still, in spite of the monotonously solemn tone, Gundolf does make distinctions which allow him to rank Goethe's works and to discriminate between and within them. Goethe appears as an "original man in a derivative world" (G, 26), constantly struggling for an assertion of the inner sources of his being against the outer impact of civilization. Gundolf draws the famous distinction between *Urerlebnisse* and *Bildungserlebnisse* (which he must have picked up from Herman Nohl). *Urerlebnis* is everything religious, titanic, and erotic; *Bildungserlebnis* is, e.g., "the German past, the encounter with Shakespeare, with classical antiquity, with Italy, with the Orient and with the whole German society of his time" (G, 27). Occasionally he allows for a third element: the setting, the house, the family, the city, and the landscape (G, 49). The *Urerlebnis* is not necessarily first chronologically. It may appear later in life or at least achieve expression only late.

Goethe's earliest writings contain nothing from which one would be able to divine his *Urerlebnis*. They are wholly dominated by *Bildungserlebnisse* (G, 35). This conflict is constantly used as standard of judgment, with the preference for the *Urerlebnis* unquestioned. Thus Gundolf can discern a relatively tame *Urerlebnis* in six poems of the Leipzig period (G, 59). In *Goetz von Berlichingen*, he criticizes the ascendency given to *Bildungserlebnis* at the expense of *Urerlebnis*; the latter being so modified as to be rendered unrecognizable (G, 124). One could put it all more simply: *Goetz* seems to Gundolf too much concerned with history and local color; and where Gundolf senses a personal concern with the guilt Goethe supposedly felt for his desertion of Friederike, he sees it as disguised in the relationship between Weislingen and Adelheide. But clearly Adelheide is conceived as an imitation of Cleopatra, a comparison (rejected by Gundolf) which should have demonstrated the absurdity of identifying the demonic Adelheide with the simple villa-girl Friederike, the daughter of a clergyman in the Alsace.

Though Gundolf rejects indignantly the model-hunting of older scholarship and the literal interpretation of Goethe's own assertion that his works are "one great confession" (G, 150), he cannot finally extricate himself from the psychologism inherent in the whole concept of *Erlebnis* derived from Dilthey. It is an appeal to immediacy, spontaneity, sincerity, which, in a criticism concerned with the value of art, is a criterion of doubtful relevance. Much of the world's poorest art is deeply felt love poetry or fervent religious and patriotic verse. In practice, Gundolf, like most Germans, prefers an art outside the Latin tradition of making, of invention and contrivance.

Fortunately the distinction of *Urerlebnis* and *Bildungserlebnis* is often replaced by another, more literary one: that between the lyrical, symbolical, and allegorical (G, 16). "Lyrical" is nearest to the core of a man's being, closest to *Urerlebnis*. *Werther* and *Tasso* (recognized by Jean-Jacques Ampère as a "gesteigerter Werther") are praised for being lyrical, for embodying Goethe's *Urerlebnis* (G, 27) in spite of their novelistic or dramatic form. In the lyric the identity of form and content is complete. The lyrical poet does not write about Spring or his beloved. He rather writes about the mood induced by external things or beings (G, 21). The lyric thus expresses the I— which would be good romantic poetics—but it must be, Gundolf insists, an I already formed or figured (G, 22). The overflow of spontaneous feeling, the lyrical cry are not enough. "Mood, atmosphere, motion must become melody, voice, word" (G, 101).

Up to the time of Goethe poets needed a symbol. Experience becomes word in Goethe, flux language. The feeling needs no image. "It is sound incarnated" (G, 102). Gundolf tried, by stylistic observations, to substantiate this assumption of a total identity of sound and meaning, form and content. He makes much of Goethe's use of epithets of motion: the adjectival use of the present participle (e.g., "heilig glühend Herz, träumende Ferne, feuchtende Fülle"), which conveys the new feeling. The same effect is achieved by activating adjectives or verbs which usually indicate only situations or functions by an added adverb of direction, as in "Berge wolkig himmelan, grüne herauf, entgegenbeben, anglühen," etc.

The word combinations in which the most heterogeneous nouns or adjectives are yoked together (e.g., "Traumglück, Nebelglanz, Wolkensteg, Scheideblick, silberprangend, schlangenwandelnd") testify not only to Goethe's love of neologisms but to the new union of sense and spirit, to the dissolution of the rational universe in a chaos of feeling. All these subtle observations (and many more) are to prove that Goethe is not writing about a subject or even expressing a definite state of mind but that somehow the state of mind is speaking itself (G, 98). There is no conflict between subject and state of mind: an irrational experience finds irrational expression (G, 99). These groping attempts to circumscribe the real novelty of Goethe's lyrics serve, on the contrary, to remind us that the lyrics do have, after all, a discernible topic. Indeed, at times, they even state an argument, trace a progression, convey a mood or an ecstasy. These ends are achieved by the techniques found in all good poetry, before and after Goethe: rhythm, imagery, symbol, myth. There is no need to appeal to woolly identifications in describing Goethe's striving for dynamic, suggestive language.

Gundolf uses the word "symbol" to mean something more specifically organized: a world of characters and actions, a myth which contrasts with the intellectual, contrived world of allegory. The distinction between symbol and allegory had been made prominently on the first page of *Shakespeare und der deutsche Geist*: "symbol expresses; is body. Allegory signifies, is sign. Allegory is conventional. Allegory is relation. Symbol is essence." (SudG, 1–2). In symbolic art the I and the world coincide; in the lyric there is only the I and no world; in allegorical art a disparity between the I and the world opens up which has to be bridged, or related or "connected" artificially (G, 24). Symbols express the motions of the I in a material originally foreign to the poet but assimilated by the creative process (G, 23). "Symbolic art" corresponds to Eliot's "objective correlative" though in Eliot the "objective correlative" is the indispensable vehicle of genuine poetic expression. For Gundolf, on the other hand, symbolic art is a stage below the highest lyrical art in which the I is identified with the world, the distinction between subject and object abolished in what seems only a grandiose gesture toward the idea of a mystical union.

Allegory is then the lowest form of art since it is contrived, artificial, intellectual. "Life and art are alogical" (SudG, 154) is Gundolf's basic presupposition. The poet is a poet because he feels and does not think, at least rationally. In practice, in the book on Goethe, Gundolf can describe *Faust* as reflecting the stages of Goethe's life (G, 766), as an organically growing work of art, while *Die natürliche Tochter* and *Achilleis* are condemned as concoctions of the brain, as lifeless academic exercises. Though he advocates like his master George a classical art and condemns everything formless, Gundolf dismisses classicist theories almost contemptuously. The concept of genre seems to him as meaningless as it was to Croce. Dante, Petrarch, Ariosto, Tasso, Rabelais, Cervantes, and Shakespeare paid no attention to traditional genres (G, 19).

The monumental portraits of Goethe and George were followed by a much smaller book on *Heinrich von Kleist* (1922), which is meant to offer a warning example. Kleist appears as enacting the tragedy of a lonely soul without nation, without gods (K, 9). Compared to Lessing he seems a blockhead, to Schiller a confused fellow, to Goethe a barbarian (K, 15). In conscious opposition to the then accepted interpretation of Kleist as a forerunner of naturalism, Gundolf sees him as an ecstatic, undisciplined visionary. *Penthesilea* becomes Kleist's most characteristic work while the tales and even *Der Prinz von Homburg* are neglected as not fitting into this picture of a man failing for lack of a community, myth, and nation (K, 45). The book on Kleist is accompanied by a series of essays (later collected into two volumes, *Romantiker* [1930] and *Romantiker: Neue Folge* [1931]) which are much more soberly descriptive and expository but show the same strong bias against anything romantic, chaotic, formless, problematic, and fanciful. The paper on Friedrich Schlegel surprises by the vehemence with which Gundolf condemns in Schlegel efforts one would think are Gundolf's or George's own: the attempt to create a new myth (Ro, 62) and to invent new terminologies (Ro, 59). The surprisingly favorable essay on Büchner plays down his social protest while admiring the mood of *Woyzeck*: "like in *Macbeth* Scotland, in *Romeo* the South, in *The Tempest* the enchanted island, free of all purposes of politics, of morals, even of reason" (Ro, 392). Büchner is a genius in the precise sense of the Latin word: "the bearer of mysterious powers of a supra- or infra-personal origin" (Ro, 395).

Gundolf thought of the two large volumes *Shakespeare: sein Wesen und Werk* (1928) as the culmination of his intimate and long familiarity with the English poet. Oddly enough the book has not, until very recently, received any close attention and has been, I believe, entirely ignored in the English-speaking world. Much of this neglect is simply due to its length, and to the difficult, often tortuous and labored style in which it is written. But difficult German books by Heidegger, Spengler, or Lukács have found translators and audiences. Gundolf's lack of impact must have deeper reasons.

Gundolf's *Shakespeare* is, first, quite unfashionably unhistorical: the dramatist is seen almost in complete isolation from his age and stage and even in conflict with his stage. Many scenes and even plays (e.g., *Henry V* and *Henry VIII*) are dismissed as concessions to the

taste of the public. Hal's rejection of Falstaff and the whole plot leading to the death of Romeo and Juliet are considered mere contrivances:
only the first part of *Henry IV* and the garden and balcony scenes in
Romeo and Juliet matter (*Sh*, I, 519, 257). *Hamlet*, we are told, was
written "for himself" as "a gloomy monologue of the passionate creative heart." Formulated in the early book (*SudG*, 35), this view was
developed at great length in the late one.

Following the general pattern first traced by Edward Dowden in
his *Shakspere* in 1875, Gundolf assumes a spiritual autobiography
behind the plays and sonnets. "His life is written in his work as precisely and clearly as Goethe's" (*Sh*, II, 287): a progression is construed
from joyous Spring or Dawn, through the tragic years of sorrow, to
the transfiguration achieved in the last romances: Shakespeare's winter
or evening. The erotic breakthrough expressed in the sonnets is considered the central experience of Shakespeare's young life. Ann Hatha-
way and the children are, I believe, never even mentioned. Anach-
ronistically, Shakespeare is interpreted consistently as a superman, a
personality in Goethe's sense who is moving beyond good and evil, a
pagan, a pantheist, a Dionysiac creator obsessed by the dark forces.
Much is, for instance, made of Gloucester's words: "As flies to wanton
boys, are we to the gods; / They kill us for their sport," a passage
which, for Gundolf, makes even the worst human crime insignificant.
Unfortunately for Gundolf's argument, Gloucester revokes this pro-
nouncement when he later speaks of the "ever-gentle gods" and "the
bounty and the benison of Heaven" and resigns saying "henceforth
I'll bear affliction."

No doubt, in the many eloquent pages of the long chapter on
King Lear, Gundolf succeeds in evoking the world of the play: the
sense of the dark forces against man; but then he bogs down in
labored sketches of all the main characters which often go astray in
reckless confusions of fiction and reality. "Cordelia," we are told in
the comment on the first scene (*Sh*, II, 235), "paralyzed by the badly
put question and the quantitative answers of her sisters, is prevented
from the immediate expression of her feeling and forced to formulate
her love quantitatively as if the frenzy and slyness of the others had
deprived her of the language of the heart." Thus, Gundolf's *Shakespeare*, in spite of its sophistication, fervor, and antithetical wit, is
actually a very old-fashioned book. It shows no interest in Shakespeare
as a man of the theater or as a contemporary of the other Elizabethan
dramatists; it is untouched by the new concern for patterns of imagery, even though Gundolf notices the recurrent animal metaphors

in *King Lear*, anticipating the much more systematic work of Caroline Spurgeon. And Gundolf quite explicitly rejects the Christian interpretation of Shakespeare, emphasizing his secularism, even paganism. He goes so far as to speak of his "praying to the unknown god" (*Sh*, II, 416). Shakespeare's tragic sense, his feeling for the powers behind the surface of nature seem to him completely unchristian. In this view, Shakespeare is made over into a contemporary of Goethe and even of Nietzsche or George.

It is difficult to avoid relegating Gundolf firmly into the past and into his setting; difficult not to see him as a propagandist for the dubious creed of George, for an inhuman hero-worship, an exclusive gesture or attitude, for a "mystery" which is hardly a mystery. One can see him also in the context of his philosophical affiliations: with Simmel and Bergson, with the whole tradition of the irrationalistic *Lebensphilosophie* first formulated, most influentially, in Germany by Wilhelm Dilthey. But we can also, in a history of literary studies, emphasize and admire Gundolf's break with the dreary positivism of the nineteenth century, his resolute rejection of externalities, the assertion, new in its time and place, of absolute values in poetry and his intensely serious concentration on what matters in the poets he studied and worshipped: their insight into the nature of man, their power of creation, and their moral and spiritual elevation. There are old truths in this gospel and we might sometimes listen to the voice of a priest in this temple.

Yale University

BIBLIOGRAPHICAL NOTE

The writings of Gundolf are quoted from these editions:
> *Shakespeare und der Deutsche Geist*, 6th ed. (Berlin, 1922), as SudG.
> *Goethe* (Berlin, 1922), as G.
> *Heinrich von Kleist* (Berlin, 1922), as K.
> *Shakespeare: sein Wesen und Werk*, 2 vols. (Berlin, 1928), as Sh.
> *Romantiker* (Berlin, 1930), as Ro.

The correspondence with George: *Stefan George-Friedrich Gundolf: Briefwechsel*, ed. Robert Boehringer and Georg Peter Landmann (Munich, 1962), is quoted as Br. *Friedrich Gundolf: Briefwechsel mit Herbert Steiner und Ernst Robert Curtius* is in the series *Castrum Peregrini* in Amsterdam, 1962–63. *Gundolf Briefe: Neue Folge* (Amsterdam, 1965) is of less interest.

Among comments I found most useful:
> Oskar Walzel's review of *Shakespeare und der deutsche Geist* in *Jahrbuch*

der deutschen Shakespeare-gesellschaft, XLVIII (1912), 259–274.

"Gundolf-heft" of Euphorion. 14. Ergänzungsheft (Leipzig, 1921) with various discussions of the book on Goethe.

Hans Rössner, Georgekreis und Literaturwissenschaft (Frankfurt, 1938). Perceptive in spite of strong Nazi tinge.

G. R. Urban, Kinesis and Stasis: A Study on the Attitude of Stefan George and his Circle to the Musical Arts (The Hague, 1962), contains a chapter on Gundolf.

Eudo C. Mason, "Gundolf und Shakespeare," in Shakespeare-jahrbuch, 1962, pp. 110–177, makes excellent points.

Victor A. Schmitz, Gundolf: Eine Einführung in sein Werk (Düsseldorf, 1965), is a sympathetic account.

REFLECTIONS ON TEACHING CRITICISM

Richard Foster

At a professional gathering not long ago, an acquaintance was telling me about his adventures with a book he had just published on a major nineteenth-century novelist. He had all but completed it some time back, he said, only to discover, on reviewing the finished work, that his critical "approach" had been all wrong; whereupon he began writing it all over again. He seemed fairly sanguine about his wasteful gaff, and it was also evident that he was serious. I knew him to be, furthermore, a sophisticated and intelligent student of literature, so I assumed that he was exaggerating for purposes of a discussion we had been having about the value of criticism courses, and that he was bringing up the matter of his book as a demonstration of their importance in the training of future scholars and critics.

I was in sympathy with his general principle about criticism courses, though about as stupefied by his anecdote as I would have been if he had told me that in setting out to buy an automobile he had unhappily ended up with a camel due to lack of expertise in the market. And yet I had been, if somewhat quizzical, respectful of similar statements made from time to time by graduate students who would explain a late paper by saying they had gotten off on the wrong "approach" to this or that writer and needed more time to go back and embark on another. No doubt my friend had overstated the circumstances of his revision out of pedagogical devotion to encouraging just such a habit of meekness before the idea of method as I had found in some of my students.

English teachers are much concerned now, in the nineteen-sixties, with criticism. Textbooks having ambitious critical structures are appearing with titles like "Approaches to Literature" (or to poetry or fiction) and introductory courses are being revamped in their wake. The history of criticism course, which in most English departments has always been offered along with the core of conventionally historical courses in literature, has been joined in the last couple of decades by courses in "modern" or "recent" criticism. Graduate seminars in critical theory have been evolved; and in certain American universities it is possible to specialize in criticism just as one might specialize, say, in linguistics or American literature. And much like poets and novelists of a generation ago, well-known critics and critics of criticism have been named to acutely specialized professorships in the art. Recently in my own institution, graduate students formally suggested that our department offer more courses in criticism, especially in modern critical methods. Younger English faculty, interested in establishing a critical methods course as a requirement for the graduate and undergraduate major, were perhaps surprised to have their cause joined not only by students but by professors of education who would like to require the same course for their prospective high school English teachers. Meanwhile, high school English departments, some of them already offering "Approaches to Literary Criticism" or something like it as an option for senior honor students, are embarking on curriculum revision under the banners of such modern theoreticians of criticism as Richards, Burke, and Frye.

Surveying the scene, even if not quite all of it is in view, one might gladden at the thought that perhaps at last literary studies are coming of age: that we may soon be able to remedy the long-standing muzziness of our activity, which makes our students' passage from teacher to teacher and course to course a continual blind adventuring into the hazardous unknown; that we may at last find objective compensations for the colleague with the tin ear or the intractable prejudice; that we may even hope to pass along the same way as such related specialties as history, philosophy, and political science where the recent elevation of positivist methodologies has greatly diminished the blurring effects of "subjectivism" and "value-questions." But best of all, sharply aware of the new multiplicity of critical tools deriving from the constructs of such thinkers as Freud, Jung, and Marx and from modern researches into all kinds of rhetorics, symbologies, and myths, we can genuinely hope, as we proceed in the task of organizing our field into an authentic discipline, to avoid the relevant danger of tyranny by monoliths.

If the presently emerging reformation in the study and teaching of literature is a long-range consequence of the impact of the New

Criticism, one of whose purposes was to make the critical study of literature more serious and substantial, I must protest, like the surprised lady in "Prufrock," that this is not what they had in mind at all. When R. P. Blackmur proclaimed the necessity, for the critic, of a variety of approaches in his confrontation with literature, his rhetoric suggested essences and subtle spirits that were to be solicited reverently, and with an infinite delicacy of tact. But the rhetoric surrounding similar imperatives of the moment suggests something quite different: matter to be "dealt with" or territories to be traversed; tool boxes and travel kits to be stocked. When an advanced student comes to me, a person known to have a special interest in criticism, and asks some such question as "Do you think a psychoanalytic approach to Dickens is valid?" I am stumped. The answer is surely not "No." Nor is it "Yes." And anything in between is an evasion of the purport of that word "valid," the word that more than any of the others in that hapless question succeeds in casting a shadow over my mind.

The New Critics' catchword descriptions of poetry as "paradox" and "irony" brought charges against them of exclusivity, narrowness, and "monism." The charges were mostly false because irrelevant. It had never been their intention to isolate and recommend any one, or any several, executive tools or methods of criticism. And they showed this in their own practice of criticism, where the languages of many conceptual structures and symbol systems were called upon to assist the labor of technical analysis. Their catchwords were meant only to indicate that poetry was dense, complex, contradictory, and yet unitary. Their purpose was not to restrict, but rather to liberate and expand the operations, in literary study, of that combination of the powers of intellect and feeling best called by the name "sensibility." Nor were they relativists either, because their whole critical enterprise was geared to maintaining and strengthening in criticism the life of just this "humanness," a value that should inform all humanistic concerns.

My purpose, however, is not to make a belated and unneeded defense of the New Critics, but rather to diagnose and perhaps prescribe for the symptoms of myopia and blank-heartedness in my colleagues and, as it seems to me, in an increasing number of my students. It will be plain from what I have said so far that I think the new disposition in literary studies generally and the teaching of criticism courses in particular must be assigned much of the responsibility for these troubles. I am not about to propose, however, that courses in criticism be played down or dropped from the curriculum. I believe, rather, that they have an important contribution to make and prob-

ably should be offered in increasing variety, but that for this very reason the pedagogical assumptions and intellectual predispositions
which now seem to govern them should be radically changed. Since
I am virtually my only resource, I must take the risk of appearing
arrogant by openly basing most of the rest of this essay on my own
opinion and practice.

My main revisionist principle is that emphasis on methodology
and relativistic objectivism, because they are opposed to sensibility and
are thus the potential enemies of literature and literary experience,
should be relegated to their properly dependent, ancillary, and at
most corrective roles in the teaching of literature and literary criticism.
No matter what the course, what we effectively "teach," most of the
time, and quite beside the point of what we may intend to teach, is
habit. And since objectivistic and methodological critical habits are
likely being more and more taught in literature courses not exclusively
governed by the concerns of literary history, courses in criticism *per
se* offer a fine opportunity for teaching the opposite and complemen-
tary humanistic habits of scepticism and sensitivity.

Among the kinds of criticism courses usually offered by English departments, the specialized—and usually advanced and rather
rarefied—course in theory and literary aesthetics would be the least
amenable to my ideal. This course is to the study of literature what
metaphysics is to the traditional study of philosophy, and no one
would wish to deny to emerging specialists with a bent toward abstract
and analytic intellection a suitable place to nourish within the pur-
view of English department training. The courses more apt to serve
the ends I envision are those in the history of criticism, which should
be made as "critical"—or "literary"—as possible, and modern criticism, which should be given a correspondingly strong historical frame-
work. For the good of the historical concern the two courses probably
ought either to be fused into one or else taught in close coordination,
with the second of them conceived, for imperative critical as well as
historical reasons, as an intensive outgrowth of the first. For the good
of the critical concern the resulting course or courses should be
restricted, as I believe, to an intensive study of selected major figures
accompanied by an assortment of the exceptional mavericks or historically unlucky who may serve not only to put the great monuments
of criticism into relief but who may sometimes induce special illumination, thanks to their brilliance or oddness or stubbornness, by making the major figures look like plodders. By taking Castelvetro and
Boileau and Lamb and Cleanth Brooks for granted, one can reserve

time for more exhaustive engagements with the titans as well as for the unusual refreshment offered by a few such normally hidden but interesting lights of criticism as Thomas Rymer, Swinburne, and Christopher Caudwell.

Early in my career as a graduate student I came under the influence of a brilliant and witty positivist professor of philosophy who taught a popular course in aesthetics. What I learned in that course, apart from some texts and concepts I hadn't run into before, was the habit of reducing the largely expressive discourse of aestheticians to a rubble of pseudo-definitions and meaningless statements. I loved the labor sanctioned by that habit because it made me feel so smart, and I panned out the dross of reductive analysis as if it were gold, heaping it up in mountainous demonstration of human reason's victimization by "emotive language." I was then also taking a genial and rather loosely managed English course in the history of criticism and decided to put some stiffening into it by handing in a blockbuster of a paper expanded from some work I had already begun in the aesthetics course. Its purpose was to demonstrate through exhaustive verbal analysis that Coleridge and Aristotle were "saying the same things," and it strongly implied that most other critical theorists probably were too. With voracious appetite I slaughtered and devoured the *Poetics* and *Rhetoric* and the *Biographia Literaria*, and the hard bright skeletons of theory and principle that remained indeed resembled each other, as most skeletons do.

I received an A on the paper—probably for the effort of mad thoroughness with which I had collected and polished my all but self-evident pebble of truth. But I also garnered a comment to the effect that though I had done the easy job well, the hard job remained to be done in the slag of discourse which, under license of the habit I had learned from my aesthetics course, I had sloughed off as "emotive terms" and "meaningless statements." It was not very long, fortunately, before I came to realize what my English professor, educated in a different generation, had probably never needed to learn: that in critical discourse, whether theoretical or practical, the *style* of its controlling logic and rhetoric is at least as important as its structure.

I almost wrote "texture" above for "style," feeling the relevance of John Crowe Ransom's description of poetry as the embodiment of a texture-structure relationship, with the former existing in excess of the latter's justifying rational requirements and becoming, thus, the cause and end of people's special kind of interest in poetry—and critics', too, if they happen also to be people. In an essay on "The Literary Criticism of Aristotle," Ransom once anthropomorphized much the same distinction in the images of two opposite kinds of minds— the "schoolmaster" (Aristotle) and the "speculative" thinker (Kant). It might be a good essay to begin a criticism course with, whether historical survey or modern, both because it encourages a sceptical rather than reverent stand before one of the most sacred monuments of criticism and because the kinds of questions it introduces could generate a workable dialectical scheme for the whole course.

"Schoolmaster." That implies definition, fixity, authority, drill, detail, and the mechanics of sorting and storing—a fair if tendentious description of the style of Aristotle's thinking, not to mention its further manifestations in the verbal style in which that thinking has come down to us. (It isn't easy to imagine Aristotle waxing witty or passionate on the lecture dais.) The style of his thinking is consonant, furthermore, with the fixed and measured nature of his world, a world in which—as we know from the stately formalism and abstraction of most of the literature and art reflecting it—terror and passion are but elements in the brutally efficient operation of simple moral equations. Emerson, who wrote the poem "Brahma," entered in his journal in 1845 some memorably sceptical words on the Greek or classical style of thinking about "Fate"—a word whose modern equivalents, for his context, might be "reality" or "existence":

The Indian system is full of fate, the Greek is not. The Greek uses the word, indeed, but in his mind the Fates are three respectable old women who spin and shear a symbolic thread,—so narrow, so limitary in the sphere allowed them, and it is with music. We are only at a more beautiful opera, or at private theatricals. But in India it is the dread reality, it is the cropping-out in our planted gardens of the core of the world; it is the abysmal Force, untameable and immense. They who wrestle with Hari see their doom in his eye before the fight begins.

With so wide a portal of inquiring scepticism thrust open, it is possible to usher in the question of just how useful the Aristotelian style of critical thinking is to understand the literature of a post-Euripidean, post-Copernican, post-Kantian, post-Jungian, world—a world bigger, less tractable, more truly mysterious (though our word is "complex") than was his. An essay on one of Shakespeare's richer plays by, say, E. E. Stoll could suggest what a great deal of the experienceable substance of literature becomes unavailable when such a style of critical thought is in force either as rule or as habit. And I see no reason why a properly motivated teacher couldn't start things off by following the same path, if he wished, with a "speculative" critic or two—raising analogous questions about, say, Coleridge and G. Wilson Knight.

From such a beginning a properly critical environment, supplementary to the historical one, can easily be built: a kind of debating room for critics, perhaps, something like E. M. Forster's imaginary salon outside time where the novelists of the ages are entertained together. The principles of construction might be put as follows: first, the intellectual principle of continual comparison and contrast of critical statements; second, the axiological principle of testing the inherent interest and worth of those statements by the trial of literature-as-experienced; and third, the—let us say "economic"—principle that from each critic's work shall be distilled answers to the questions, What are the critic's conceptions of the nature of literature, the function of literature, and the form of the creative process? This last principle is intended to insure that something besides a habit is taught; the first to encourage thinking to take precedence over sorting and storing; and the second to assure that neither critical thinking nor knowledge about criticism shall be allowed to seem ends in themselves apart from or superior to a more general regard for the value of literature.

I should like to make a modest test case, a small model of possible procedure, out of Dr. Johnson. Students will know that he is the archetypal neo-classicist. And they are likely to have a living if somewhat over-vivid image of him as a man, too—the solemn, large-gestured hero, in his Jovian gestures and trumpetings, of the last act of the drama of English Augustanism. Probably they will know the tenth chapter of *Rasselas*; but if doors are to be kept open, best not begin with that handy condensed guide to the Rules. Better to begin with Johnson as practical critic probing literature with the sharp weaponry of his judgment. If the well-known passage on the Metaphysical Poets from the life of Cowley is chosen, comparison can be initiated right away with Eliot's equally famous essay on the same subject. Students will note that the striking likeness of perception in the two essays stops at the border of judgment: Johnson dispraises what Eliot praises. What is missing, then, from the earlier critic's approach that is present in Eliot's? Arriving at a reasonably subtle answer to this question might take some time. But what should very soon become evident, and perhaps as a small surprise to stock presuppositions, is that Johnson does not judge easily and mechanically. Though he invokes the sacred name of Aristotle as "the father of criticism," and though the canon of neo-classical principles and rules is inherently restrictive, Johnson uses his inheritance only as a basis or beginning for a complex critical activity. No mere proprietor of a method, as favorable comparison with Eliot's supple essay will tend to show, could have produced the shrewd, witty, expressive, characterizing distinctions of which Johnson's essay is made. Like Eliot, Johnson has read the poems feelingly, submitted his experience of them to the scrutiny of an acutely attuned dissective intelligence, and synthesized all the results in a definitive act of judgment. This conclusion can be reinforced by considering Johnson's judgments of other writers—Milton, Gray, Richardson, and Fielding—all of which valuations, whatever their weight or direction, grow out of responsive experiencing of the writers' works. As a critic of Shakespeare, Johnson, like Pope, is an exponent of neo-classicism. But where Pope is the impersonal if stylish servant of it as an absolute system of norms, Johnson makes the system serve his perception as a dependent, and often relative, vocabulary of personal judgment. Pope's critical "errors" are historically predicated blind spots; but Johnson's usually turn out to be viable expressive insights detachable from their vehicle of judgment. Pope, then, is a graceful artifact adorning a shelf in that timeless hospitality room for critics where Johnson lives, breathes, and makes himself heard as a man. And a return encounter with Eliot in this environment will tend to show that what "lacks" from Johnson's treatment of the metaphysical poets, is, curiously, a kind of limitation in Eliot—an intention to put criticism at the disposal of a program for rejuvenating traditional Christian culture—which in its essential historicity is far more like Pope's limitations than any of Johnson's.

Once an atmosphere of real inquiry has been created, perhaps by means of some such comparative undertakings as I have suggested here, one can usefully return to the handy guide, *Rasselas* X. Is it that after all? Is it really the same kind of thing that Pope's "Essay on Criticism" is? Flanking *Rasselas* X and the "Essay" respectively with "The Vanity of Human Wishes" and "The Essay on Man"—the former as darkly redolent with personal feeling as is the latter glittering with a finely articulated display of conventional gestures—should help to elicit a just and discriminating negative. Seen in the larger context of his work, even so stock-seeming a piece as *Rasselas* X seems to breathe the atmosphere of Johnson's personal vision, a vision that, if it is Christian-stoical in moral rigors, is tragic in substance. While it may not be the concern of the criticism course to "rank" Johnson definitively, it certainly is its concern to discriminate the qualities that give him an identity and value for criticism larger than that of a cultural artifact. His final claim to greatness as a critic has nothing to do with his having lasted, his being typical, or his having mastered certain critical methods and skills, but rather with his transcendence of these limits through his sure exercise of a gift of sensitivity nurtured and colored far more deeply by the natural substance of his temperament and character as a man than by any conceptual system forced upon him by history.

Addressing the terminal questions at this point will suggest possibilities for further comparative thinking. Johnson's idea of the nature (or structure) of literature is never explicitly stated, but it can be readily deduced from *Rasselas* X and his practical criticism. It is simple, traditional, "Horatian": literature is a moral substructure fleshed out with experienceable particulars intended to generate morally appropriate and thus useful patterns of feeling. Simple and unquestioned as this idea of the nature of literature is, Johnson's humane management of it makes it a house capable, nevertheless, of accommodating many and various mansions. At the very least it suggests his relevance to Wordsworth, thus providing some fuel for later discussion of the differences in theory between Wordsworth and Coleridge. And it gives such more recent critics as Babbitt and Leavis and Winters a suggestive context of tradition. To Johnson the function of literature, following from its nature, is moral. Spiritual and social consequences are implicit in it, but as secondary by-products of its prime function as a source of strength-giving "wisdom" for the individual. A precursor, then, of Arnold and Eliot, Johnson stands opposed to Poe, Mallarmé, and Susanne Langer, and interestingly illuminates the complex mediative position of Coleridge and such Coleridge inheritors as Burke and Richards. In *Rasselas* X the creative process is defined as essentially "rational." The poet, imbued with a living sense of the human condition, studies and stores representative facts of nature and human life and composes them, under the impetus of consequent natural feeling, into significant images of man's nature and fate—a process similar to that illustrated in practice by Wordsworth and recommended as theory by such naturalists and realists as Howells and Zola.

Finding such grounds of likeness as these should lead back again, of course, to revived understanding of the old familiar discriminations whose edges may have become blurred by academic cliché and stock response. But more important still, it should suggest the subtlety, largeness, and flexibility of mind natural to the true critic—thus tend-ing to teach the most necessary critical habits along with knowledge about the ideas and judgments of a particular critic who might be considered a model for the calling.

A device I have found useful for sustaining this sort of speculative inquiry and comparison in the criticism course is the assignment of brief (one page or less) and frequent (weekly, or daily if the group is small) written reactions to the critics up for discussion. With the timeless room as a setting for unfettered dialogue, almost any kind of statement that is intelligent, sensitive, or interesting—from small quibbles over a detail of interpretation to brave thrusts at judgment or theory—will serve the ends of the course.

A more familiar writing assignment in criticism courses is to have students apply some "method"—Aristotelian, Freudian, mythographic, whatever—to some selected work or works of literature. Because such projects, even when well done, usually result in exercises rather than criticism, and thus promote methodism at the expense of sensitivity, I think they should be assigned with special care. When students are in danger of succumbing to a schoolmaster critic, for example, I ask them to handle the model performance with dispatch so that they can put most of their effort into determining the limitations of the critic's method—identifying those organic constituents of the work which the method would lead the critic to distort, reduce, or ignore. When students choose a critic of the ingenious or idiosyncratic kind, I ask them to try for the style as well as the substance of his performance—the humor and delicacy of Burke or Empson, the boldness and wit of Lawrence, the elegance of Eliot. In order to discourage results that are dully routine it seems best, too, to urge students to confront their critics with works that will pose unusual problems for them and thus generate critical sparks of some intensity: apply Aristotle to *Waiting for Godot* rather than *Mourning Becomes Electra*, for example, or Henry James to Robbe-Grillet.

But the importance of this classic assignment should probably be rather played down in relation both to the short assignments in critical dialogue and to a third kind of writing assignment which I believe, keeping in view my notion of the proper ends of the course, can be the most interesting and useful of all: the assignment of a critical essay—not a "study" ("Motifs of Light and Darkness in Conrad's Fiction"), nor an introduction ("Conrad's *Nostromo*"), but a critical essay. Since studies and introductions are the kinds of papers literature students most often write, prohibition of such efforts tends to bring on more than the usual amount of consternation over what it is that the instructor "wants." But such a reaction, sad as it is, has its uses, for clarification of the assignment can be made into yet another occasion for teaching humane, as distinct from scientific, critical habits. In order to reduce to a minimum the temptations of pedantic rope-dancing, I ask students to think of the paper they are to write as an effort at definitive persuasion addressed to an audience whose perception must be sharpened and widened and feelings energized so that its judgment will be altered. I suggest that they do one of three things: question and readjust the conventional estimation of some under-criticized but overrated classic; do the same—the readjustment to have an upward direction this time—with some neglected work by an established master; or write an essay in discovery of the larger literary merits of some minor or marginal writer or work. Suggestions of typical projects will help. For the first, one might propose, for example, a revaluative examination of the possible structural, and thus thematic, incoherence of *Hamlet*, or hint at the sentimentality of some late Henry James. But because this assignment seems to authorize intemperate splurges of critical iconoclasm, students must of course be reminded that tradition's valuations, are not usually wrong, but rather only stock or over-simple, and that the aim of reappraisal should not be to destroy them, but to subtilize them into life. Some models can be brought forward: Lawrence on Hawthorne (perhaps set off against Matthiessen-Melville on Hawthorne); or C. S. Lewis on Donne (perhaps set off against Eliot on Donne). For the second project one might suggest something like Poe's *The Narrative of Arthur Gordon Pym* or Vladimir Nabokov's *Pnin* or the poems of Ford Madox Ford. And for the third every instructor is likely to have a large private hoard of lost or hidden gems that he would like to reveal for admiration and appraisal.

Already warned against mechanicalness, students should be encouraged to give to their readings, no matter how systematic they may be, a warmth of personal commitment. But if they are still not quite sure what is "wanted," a last exhibition of prime examples, as varied as possible, can be made available. My own choices for such a purpose might include Allen Tate on Poe, Lionel Trilling on Dreiser, and G. M. Young on the poems of Thomas Hardy. Though the first is known as a New Critic, the second as a "Freudian," and the third was both a professional historian and a self-styled "Victorian," students can be shown that the effectiveness of each critic's essay derives not from some identifying approach or method or milieu, but rather from the critics' capacities to live sensitively and responsively as whole human beings in the medium of the works they have chosen to write about. As a last precaution I ask students to give me short, clear prospectuses for the essays they want to write, these providing a basis for preliminary conferences about the uncertain and needy cases.

Criticism courses, whether historical or modern, can be among the most valuable offered by English departments. They can provide a kind of literary history from the "inside"—something that most historically oriented literature courses do not provide. And they can help turn students into critics—which is the real end, perhaps, of all courses in literature. I doubt that most courses in criticism as presently conceived and taught in American universities and colleges further these ends because they are built on a quasi-technical (frequently euphemized as "philosophical") mistrust of common sense and sensitivity in regard to literature. Such a reflexive mistrust—alas that the truism should prove to be true—is an expression of the current ascendance of science and expertism over humanism.

Method is "machinery." And skill in method comes by "training"—a word employed by Newman to make a distinction between education and something that was not only not education but perhaps close to its opposite. Even if methods are called "approaches" and even if the approaches are defined as "partial," "provisional," "relative" items of lumber in a large warehouse of pluralistic methodological possibility, the teacher of criticism as method is implying, really, because the products of training and machinery are predictable, that he has nothing to learn from criticism, including that written by his students. He *is* that warehouse; and his purpose is to provide the machinery and the principles of construction for smooth-running critical factories. The imagery is lurid and vulgar, but there is no other available that fits the case. It is the right kind of imagery to express the present mood in the teaching of criticism.

But of course there is no such person—yet—as I have described. In fact the most method-bound teachers are still human enough to be pleased, even delighted, when they find themselves suddenly learning something new about literature from a gifted student. I have been pleased by this experience most often when reading the essays written for my criticism courses. I take a little credit for this result to myself for persisting especially hard there, often to the despair of students who find that their hard-won training and the elaborate critical machineries at their disposal are of little avail in giving the teacher "what he wants," in teaching my conviction that much knowledge, at least knowledge about such things as critical theories and methods, can be far more dangerous, in the practice of literary criticism, than a little or none at all. To discourage the rough beast *Criticus Propaedeuticus* from establishing his barbarous rule in our and our students' minds is perhaps the first obligation of the teacher of literary criticism in this latter day.

University of Minnesota

INDEX